System Safety:
HAZOP and Software HAZOP

System Safety:
HAZOP and Software HAZOP

Felix Redmill
Redmill Consultancy, London, UK

Morris Chudleigh
Cambridge Consultants Limited, Cambridge, UK

and

James Catmur
Arthur D. Little Limited, Cambridge, UK

JOHN WILEY & SONS
Chichester · New York · Weinheim · Brisbane · Singapore · Toronto

Other Wiley Editorial Offices

John Wiley & Sons, Inc., 605 Third Avenue,
New York, NY 10158-0012, USA

WILEY-VCH Verlag GmbH, Pappelallee 3,
D-69469 Weinheim, Germany

Jacaranda Wiley Ltd, 33 Park Road, Milton,
Queensland 4064, Australia

John Wiley & Sons (Asia) Pte Ltd, 2 Clementi Loop #02-01,
Jin Xing Distripark, Singapore 129809

John Wiley & Sons (Canada) Ltd, 22 Worcester Road,
Rexdale, Ontario M9W 1L1, Canada

Library of Congress Cataloging-in-Publication Data
Redmill, Felix.
    System safety : HAZOP and software HAZOP / Felix Redmill, Morris Chudleigh, James Catmur.
        p.   cm.
    Includes bibliographical references and index.
    ISBN 0-471-98280-6 (alk. paper)
    1. Industrial safety — Management.   I. Chudleigh, Morris II. Catmur, James.   III. Title.
T55.R43   1999
620.8′6 — dc21   98-55085
                                                            CIP
British Library Cataloguing in Publication Data
A catalogue record for this book is available from the British Library

ISBN   0-471-98280-6

Produced from PostScript files supplied by Hilite, Southampton, based on electronic files supplied by the authors.
Printed and bound in Great Britain by Antony Rowe Ltd, Eastbourne
This book is printed on acid-free paper responsibly manufactured from sustainable forestry, in which at least two trees are planted for each one used for paper production.

Contents

Preface

Hazard and operability study (HAZOP) is perhaps the most powerful technique for the identification and analysis of hazards. Developed in the chemical industry, it has for some time been a key tool in carrying out safety analysis in the process industries, and it has also been employed in other industries, including railway and nuclear.

With the emergence of standards which demand an understanding of the risks posed by a system, there has been a spread to all industries of the need for safety analysis based on thorough hazard identification. Importantly, the use of software-based systems in almost all control applications has necessitated the transfer of safety technology from its traditional industries to the field of software engineering.

So the need to understand and carry out hazard identification and analysis has grown substantially in recent years.

This book provides both a thorough course in HAZOP for beginners and descriptions of particular problems and applications for more experienced practitioners. Indeed, its explanation of the control of the HAZOP process may lead many practitioners to understand why their less rigorous application of the technique has not been as efficient or effective as they had expected. The structured form of the book also makes it ideal as a reference text.

After the introduction of the first chapter, the second places HAZOP in the context of the overall management of safety. Chapter 3 then gives an overview of the technique for two reasons; first, to provide the introduction which newcomers require in order to understand the subsequent chapters, and second, to provide a common understanding of the process itself for all readers. Chapters 4 to 10 then offer a step-by-step course and reference manual of the process.

The subsequent chapters then give additional information and guidance (they may be considered as 'advanced instruction'). Chapter 11 advises on when it is most appropriate to use the technique in the life of a system and shows how it is complementary to fault modes and effects analysis (FMEA). Chapter 12 deals with difficulties which can arise in conducting HAZOP, Chapter 13 tackles the problematic task of carrying out the technique on systems which include a human, and Chapter 14 addresses the HAZOP of a system in a changing environment, using as an example a moving train. Chapter 15 then provides examples of HAZOPs of programmable electronic systems.

Finally, Chapter 16 offers advice and ideas on introducing HAZOP into an organisation and auditing and improving its use.

We believe this coverage to be thorough and hope that is provides not only a sound basis for learning the HAZOP technique but also a reference source for its use.

We would like to thank Kevin Geary for his help and support, and Barry Hebbron and Gordon Sellars for taking time to criticise drafts of this book; their comments and suggestions have been invaluable. We would also like to thank our colleagues in Arthur D. Little and the clients we have worked with, all of whom have helped us in our thinking in the field of HAZOP.

1
Introduction

HAZOP (hazard and operability study) is a technique for identifying and analysing the hazards and operational concerns of a system. It has been in use for many years, but, although it is established internationally as one of the foremost hazard identification techniques, it has remained until recently almost entirely confined to the process (chemical, pharmaceutical, oil and gas) industries. Yet, it is universally applicable.

In spite of being an established technique, HAZOP is not applied consistently and often not carried out effectively. The title 'HAZOP' has been accorded to almost any attempt to identify hazards, often when the most casual approaches were employed. In many cases, while believing that they have employed the method correctly, exponents have achieved poor results at high cost, and deduced that the method is unsuitable — whereas, in fact, they have often failed in a key area, that of its management. The tendency to use the technique incorrectly has not been helped by the fact that the literature on the subject has been sparse and, like the technique itself, confined mainly to the process industries. HAZOP is easy to understand and apparently easy to apply, but, being based on teamwork, it requires careful management and control. Without this, there is certain to be a loss of both effectiveness and efficiency. This point cannot be over-emphasised, and it will recur throughout this book.

One purpose of this book is therefore to present a clear description of

HAZOP for all who wish to understand the method, whether they are newcomers wishing to learn it or experienced practitioners wanting to improve their use of it. Another purpose is to explain the importance of the formalism of the process, so that its use becomes more consistent and more effective. If *ad hoc* studies, inadequately controlled and not conducted in accordance with clear rules, were not styled as 'HAZOP', confusion would be removed from the process of hazard identification. Then, given that the identification of hazards is the foundation of the effective management of safety (see Chapter 2), safer systems and plant would result.

With the rapid increase in the number of safety-critical software-based systems (referred to as 'programmable electronic systems' or PES) throughout industry, there has been an urgent need to transfer safety engineering techniques from their traditional fields of application (mainly in nuclear power and process industries) to the development and operation of PES. For example, PES are currently employed in civil and military aircraft, road, rail, air and marine transport, medical systems, water treatment, the control of industrial processes, power generation, and mining, all of which are either safety-critical or have safety implications. It is therefore essential for the hazards associated with intended systems to be identified and analysed before the systems are designed, and to be eliminated or reduced before the systems are brought into service. So, a further, and crucial, purpose of the book is to explain the application of HAZOP to PES.

Achieving safety in PES development involves the integration of safety engineering into software and hardware engineering. In operation, it demands a greater awareness of the safety implications of the systems in question and, more generally, a safety culture in the organisations responsible for them. With the intention of supporting the management of safety in system development, Committee 65A of the International Electrotechnical Committee (IEC) has developed a draft standard, IEC 61508 [IEC 98], one feature of which is that it identifies safety engineering techniques suitable for use at the various stages of a system's life cycle — and one of these is HAZOP.

In attempting to apply HAZOP to the hazard analysis of PES, problems have arisen, not because the fundamental principles are inapplicable but because PES require interpretations and additional advice which have not normally been necessary in the process industries. Some problems have led to failure of the attempt to apply the technique, and others have appeared simply to make it difficult to employ.

In our own applications of HAZOP to computer-based systems, the present authors had encountered difficulties and, in many cases, had devised ways of overcoming them. Then, in a contract to prepare a guideline on the technique for the UK Ministry of Defence, we spent a considerable time carrying out further research [Redmill 97]. We polled industry to find those with experience in applying HAZOP to PES, held workshops to identify, assess and discuss the problems which we had experienced in doing so, examined our own experience of solving those problems, carried out further study, drafted the guideline, and then sought industry's comments on it. Later, the authors revised the document in the light of industry's comments to produce the Interim Defence Standard 00-58 [MOD 96].

The difficulties in applying HAZOP to PES were consistent across industries and took the form of six broad problems:

- What was the appropriate team structure and what should the roles of the team members be?
- Which design representations were applicable, and were there any which were not?
- What attributes should be used in applying the technique?
- There was considerable confusion as regards guide words. It was not clear whether the traditional guide words were applicable, and new guide words were frequently being introduced in order to cope with difficulties. The recurrent question was whether there was a set of guide words which could be used in all cases or whether HAZOP teams would forever have to invent new ones in every situation.
- What method of recording the HAZOP results was appropriate?
- It was recognised that HAZOP was invaluable in identifying hazards early in a project. But it was also known that there was a need to continue safety analysis, and therefore to identify new or changed hazards, throughout a system's life. So there was confusion as to when in the life cycle it was appropriate to apply HAZOP.

In addressing our purpose of writing a book which explains the application of HAZOP to PES, we have paid particular attention to these issues. Not only does the book expand on the succinct guideline produced for the Ministry of Defence, but it also provides further details based on the authors' subsequent trials and industrial use of HAZOP on PES.

The principles and examples presented in this book are not exclusive to any particular application of HAZOP. The technique is now being used more and more widely (albeit not necessarily effectively or efficiently), for example, on mechanical and electrical systems as well as chemical plant and PES. Thus, an additional aim of this book is to show how to use HAZOP in these areas, by applying the principles and by extending the PES and other examples.

1.1   WHAT IS HAZOP?

HAZOP is a methodical investigation of the hazards and operational problems to which the plant or system being studied could give rise (the term 'plant' is prevalent in some industries, but 'system' will be used throughout this book). Because of its safety engineering objectives, this book focuses on the use of HAZOP for the identification and analysis of hazards, but it is also relevant to operational problems. Hazards can result from a 'deviation from design intent' (the intention of the designer). Such deviations can occur in either a component of the system or an interaction between components of the system. The first step, that of hazard identification, is to identify a possible hazardous deviation from design intent. The next, that of hazard analysis, is to investigate the deviation's possible causes and consequences.

A HAZOP is carried out not on the physical system itself, but on a representation of it — the 'design representation' — which must be documented. The design representation may be at a more or less detailed level and in any one of a number of symbolic forms, from simple block diagrams to formal mathematical notation. Though it is preferable for it to be pictorial, this is not mandatory, and there is no evidence to suggest that any design representations preclude the use of HAZOP, though some may present more difficulties than others. The important thing is that the investigation must be based on a design representation which exists and which is understandable to the study team.

A HAZOP is carried out by a team (never by an individual), and the selection of appropriate team members is crucial. The control of the process, and therefore the leadership of the study team, is key to its success. If HAZOP is treated as merely a technical process, it is unlikely to be employed effectively. Weak or ineffectual leadership, resulting in poor control, has led many studies to fail to uncover hazards, even though the study teams have included appropriate experts.

1.2   THE CONTEXT OF HAZOP IN SAFETY ANALYSIS

Producing a safe product and operating it safely are not 'one-off' activities. They depend on a continuous attention to safety throughout the product's life cycle. One aspect of attention to safety is that of a safety culture, wherein everyone is aware of safety issues, alert to problems which might cause a breach of safety, and ready to do whatever is practical to maintain safety. Another aspect of attention to safety is 'safety analysis', which is the application of safety engineering techniques throughout the life cycle, to ensure the achievement of an acceptable level of safety and to demonstrate this so as to assure others (such as management, independent assessors and customers) that the required level of safety has been achieved.

To be objectively carried out and assessed, safety analysis must commence with the identification of the hazards posed by the system in question. These must then be analysed so as to determine the risks associated with them. One of the foremost techniques for the identification of hazards and the analysis of their causes and consequences is HAZOP, so this technique is often employed early in the safety analysis process. Then, as the life cycle proceeds and the system changes through specification, re-specification, design, correction, and onwards towards operation, new hazards and causes may be introduced, and hazards and causes not previously recognised may become identifiable because of the increased detail available. So it is often appropriate to carry out HAZOP at several points in the life cycle, the technique thus contributing to an increasing confidence that the required level of safety is being approached.

Adequate confidence in system safety cannot be achieved by the use of any single technique, but only by carrying out a full series of safety analyses, extending over the entire life of the system and including the application of a range of techniques. Ideally, confidence in the system's safety increases as the safety analysis proceeds, and should have achieved a defined acceptable level by the time the developed system is ready to be brought into service. Even then the safety analysis should not end. Safety should be reviewed throughout the operational life of a system, particularly when changes to the system or its environment are contemplated or implemented, and here again HAZOP is an invaluable tool.

1.3   THIS BOOK

As mentioned in Section 1.1, there are three main purposes to this book:

- To present a clear description of HAZOP for all who wish to understand the method, whether they are newcomers or experienced practitioners;
- To explain the importance of the formalism of the process, so that its use becomes more consistent and more effective;
- To explain the application of HAZOP to software-based systems and thus, by example, other fields in which it has not hitherto been employed.

In the book HAZOP is described in a generic manner, suitable to application in any industry and to any type of system. At the same time, by explaining the application of the technique to programmable electronic systems, and by providing examples based on them, the book identifies the problems in applying the technique to new areas and technologies and explains how to overcome them. It thus takes the subject further than previous introductory texts such as [Kletz 92] and [CIA 77] and is both a learning text and a reference manual.

Chapters 2 and 3 provide the context for understanding HAZOP. First, Chapter 2 expands on Section 1.3, explaining how the technique fits into the life-cycle process of safety analysis. Then, Chapter 3 offers an overview of the technique itself. This overview is essential to the novice reader for it provides the context and framework into which the details later to be presented will fit. These details are given in Chapters 4 to 10 and are structured so as to provide a course for the beginner. Each chapter presents one of the significant aspects of HAZOP.

Following this extensive description of the technique and its application, Chapter 11 offers advice on when in the life cycle HAZOP is likely to be most effective, Chapters 12 to 14 provide details of applications which offer particular difficulties, and Chapter 15 gives detailed examples of the application of HAZOP to PES. Finally, Chapter 16 considers the introduction of the technique into an organisation, auditing its use, and improving its effectiveness and efficiency.

2

The Role of Hazard Identification in the Management of Safety

This chapter briefly reviews the management of safety and the part that hazard identification plays in it. The purpose is to place the HAZOP technique for hazard identification in context rather than to give definitive guidance on the whole area of safety management and analysis. Readers who wish for more detail, particularly in relation to computer-based systems, may refer to Neil Storey [Storey 96] and to the other documents referred to in this chapter.

The whole fabric of our society depends on our ability to design, build and operate a vast number of artifacts. Unfortunately, the failure of many of the things we build can lead to accidents and harm. They may be affected not only by system failure, but also by an inattention to safety matters during the development and operation of reliable systems. We need to design, build and operate artifacts such that they are acceptably safe, and this can be done only by proper attention to safety issues throughout their lives.

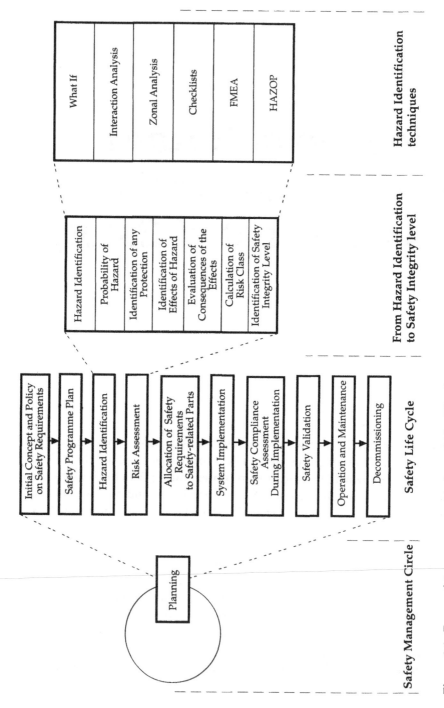

Figure 2.1: From safety management to hazard identification

To introduce these principles, this chapter discusses a number of themes, starting from the general issues of safety management and then looking at particular points in more detail. The following subjects will be introduced in turn:

- Safety is an attribute that can and should be managed proactively within a defined framework of activities;
- There is a defined safety life cycle covering the development of systems and products;
- Hazard identification and risk assessment have an important place in the safety life cycle;
- HAZOP is one of the leading techniques in hazard identification and complements some other common techniques.

The relationships between these themes are represented in Figure 2.1 and expanded on in the remainder of the chapter.

2.1   SAFETY CAN AND SHOULD BE MANAGED

This section introduces two fundamental ideas to help explain the issues concerned with managing safety:

- The concept of tolerability of safety risk;
- That a traditional 'management circle' applies to the management of safety.

2.1.1 Tolerability of Safety Risk

The identification of hazards is an important early step in being able to design, build and operate safe systems. But what is safe? What is a hazard?

A widely used definition of safety is one given in MIL-STD-882C [DOD 93], a standard produced by the US Department of Defense: 'freedom from those conditions that can cause death, injury, occupational illness, or damage to or loss of equipment or property, or damage to the environment'.

A hazard is defined in Interim Defence Standard 00-56 [MOD 95] as: 'a physical situation, often following from some initiating event, that can lead to an accident'.

Given these definitions, it is very important to recognise that there is no such thing as absolute safety — there are hazards (and hence risks) involved in all human activities — and the purpose of most safety management activities is to reduce the risk of harm to a tolerable level.

The required level of safety depends on a number of factors, including the severity of injury, the number of people exposed to the risk, societal perception, guidelines from regulatory authorities, standards in the industry concerned, international agreements, expert advice and legal requirements. Within society we have differing views of the safety risks we are willing to take. In the UK, people accept that thousands are killed in road accidents each year, but would be horrified if there were an equivalent number of deaths from rail or air transport. One explanation is that on the roads we each feel 'in control', and so are willing to tolerate a higher degree of risk to our life than if we entrusted control to others (or maybe we do not even perceive that there is a significant risk). There is also a general feeling that we are more tolerant of a single life being lost in each of thirty accidents over a given period of time than of thirty people being killed in one accident during the same period.

Some recent research in the UK by Mike Jones-Lee [Jones-Lee 95] suggests that this is not people's perception and it is the total number of deaths that affects how we feel about risk to life. Interested readers are referred to the work of Jones-Lee.

The media and politicians also have a large effect on how risks are perceived. The amount of coverage given to an accident or a safety issue by the press affects public opinion, as does the interest taken by politicians and the subsequent media attention given to that interest.

Thus, the effort invested in reducing a safety risk in an emotive area where there is strong public or media pressure may need to be much greater than the effort based on a purely objective evaluation of the safety risks.

In recent years the Health and Safety Executive (HSE) in the UK has done much work (see, for example, [HSE 89]), to develop a philosophy of tolerability of risk, where risks are put into one of three classes:

- The risk is small enough to be trivial or broadly acceptable (negligible);
- The risk lies between negligible and intolerable and should be reduced to the lowest level practicable, after carrying out a trade-off between the benefits of reducing the risk and the cost of any reduction (tolerable);
- The risk is so great that it must be refused altogether (intolerable).

When the risk lies between negligible and intolerable, the ALARP (as low as reasonably practicable) principle is used. Here the risk is tolerable only if further risk reduction is impracticable or the cost of risk reduction is grossly disproportionate to the improvement gained — see Figure 2.2. The

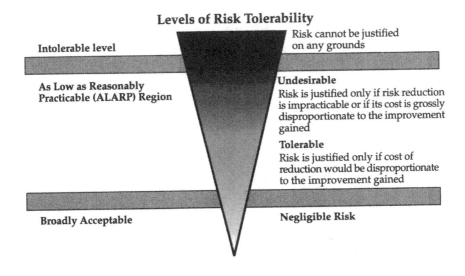

Levels of Risk Tolerability

Intolerable level — Risk cannot be justified on any grounds

As Low as Reasonably Practicable (ALARP) Region

Undesirable
Risk is justified only if risk reduction is impracticable or if its cost is grossly disproportionate to the improvement gained

Tolerable
Risk is justified only if cost of reduction would be disproportionate to the improvement gained

Broadly Acceptable — **Negligible Risk**

Figure 2.2: Levels of risk tolerabililty and the ALARP principle

HSE quantifies the levels of individual risk. As an example, the individual risk of someone dying from a lightning strike in the UK is about one in 10 million per year and would thus be considered a negligible risk.

The ALARP principle has been around since the UK Health and Safety at Work Act in 1974 [HASAW 74] and it gained wide awareness following the Cullen report into the Piper Alpha oil rig disaster in the North Sea in the late 1980s [Cullen 90]. The concept of carrying out a cost-benefit trade-off as a part of risk analysis has become established in the UK and a number of other countries and is now to be found in emerging standards such as [IEC 98].

2.1.2   A Safety Management Process

Managing a system's development so as to ensure that it is adequately safe is similar to managing other activities. A well-known model, used in many areas of management, is the 'management circle'. An application of this to the management of health and safety by the HSE [HSE 92] is shown in Figure 2.3.

Here there are six (generic) activities shown in an iterative loop. In the context of health and safety of an organization, the generic activities cover

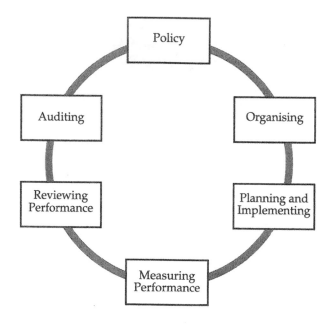

Figure 2.3: A management circle

both the health and safety of those working in the organization and the safety of systems and products designed and produced. They may be summarised as follows:

- Policy (the guiding principles of what we need to do): this activity includes the processes of creating a policy on safety, obtaining management commitment throughout the organization and defining principles. Policy should define the principles aimed at the preservation of physical and human resources and the reduction of financial losses and liabilities. The principles will influence all activities and decisions, including the design and delivery of products and systems.

- Organising (who should do it): assigning responsibilities for safety to parts of the organization, defining authority and job descriptions, and developing control methods. Organizations which achieve high safety standards create a positive culture of involvement at all levels and have good communication and training to enable everyone to make an effective contribution. The aim is not simply to avoid accidents but to motivate and empower people to work safely.

- Planning and implementing (how to do it and doing it): the process of setting objectives, producing standards, guidelines and procedures, generating plans, prioritizing activities and carrying them out in an effective manner. The aim is to manage the risks created by all activities, including the building of systems and products (and of course ensuring that the resulting systems and products will be safe in operation). Risk assessment methods are used to set priorities and objectives so as to eliminate some hazards and to reduce the risks arising from others. Wherever possible, risks are eliminated by careful selection and design of facilities, equipment and processes. This aspect of the development of systems and products is expanded on in the remaining sections of this chapter.

- Measuring performance (how well it was done): includes measuring against predetermined standards to detect when and where action is needed to improve performance. Success is assessed through active self-monitoring: looking at the 'hard' things of premises, plant, substances and computer hardware, and the 'soft' things of people, procedures and computer software. Accidents or incidents show a failure of control and these require thorough investigation. The identification of underlying causes and their implications for the design and operation of the safety management system is a key part of this measuring activity.

- Reviewing performance (how to do things better): reviews corporate performance based on learning from all relevant experience. Commitment to continuous improvement needs constant development of policies, approaches to implementation and techniques of risk control. Those organizations which attain high standards review performance by internal reference to key performance indicators and by external comparison with other businesses.

- Auditing (to give an independent view): assesses the validity and reliability of the management planning and control systems. It supports monitoring by giving information on the implementation and effectiveness of plans and performance standards and the arrangements for all the other activities in the circle. It is carried out by competent people who are independent of the area being audited. Auditing provides the 'feedback loop' to enable the organization to maintain and develop its ability to manage risks to the fullest possible extent.

Figure 2.4: Overall safety life cycle

2.2   THE SAFETY LIFE CYCLE FOR SYSTEMS AND PRODUCTS

This section expands on the planning and implementation step of the safety activities introduced above, by defining a system development safety life cycle (see Figure 2.4). This takes elements from two of the emerging standards in the area of safety ([MOD 95], [IEC 98]) and is the second column of activities in Figure 2.1.

The life cycle phases of Figure 2.4 are briefly explained as follows:

- The concept phase is to develop an understanding of the functions which the system must carry out, the environment within which it must operate, and some of the possible design approaches.

- The safety programme plan defines the management and technical activities that will be used to assess the level of safety required of the system and to ensure that the safety-related system achieves and maintains the required level of functional safety. The plan should be produced at the beginning of the system life cycle and reviewed at regular intervals.

- Hazard identification is a process which should be started at the earliest possible stage and which (although shown as a single item on the figure) continues throughout the system life cycle. It identifies the hazards which might arise during construction, installation, operation, maintenance and disposal of the system. HAZOP is an important technique for use in this step.

- Risk assessment is the process of analysing the identified hazards to assess the risks arising from them (in either a qualitative or a quantitative way) and checking whether these risks are tolerable. Action must be taken to reduce the overall risks arising from the consequences of each hazard to a tolerable level. This gives rise to requirements for the safety integrity level (discussed below in Section 2.3) for the system.

- The safety requirements for the system are then allocated to the various parts of the system and the overall architecture is reviewed to ensure that the risk will be reduced to an acceptable level. In general, simple technology should be used to implement the safety functions as this reduces the overall complexity. For example, a decision to implement a particular safety function with a simple mechanical interlock rather than in software might avoid the need for the control software to be safety-related.

- The safety-related parts are then implemented to meet their safety requirements.

- Assessment of the safety-related parts is carried out to check for compliance with the safety requirements. A mixture of analysis and auditing techniques is used.

- Safety validation is used to provide confidence that the claimed safety characteristics of the system have been achieved in practice and to resolve any problems arising from the verification.

- During the operation and maintenance of the system it is necessary to maintain system safety. Any differences in the environment of use, the way in which the system is used, and changes to the system itself, should be analysed to evaluate their effects on safety.

- In decommissioning, the safety of the system must be managed. Thus an assessment of the impact of the decommissioning should be made. This will tend to use hazard and risk analysis to determine the level of safety-related work that needs to be carried out during the decommissioning activity .

It should be recognised that the majority of real system developments (and their associated safety activities) do not totally follow the linear life cycle shown in Figure 2.4. There is a need for iteration as the requirements of the system and the most effective means of achieving those requirements will evolve over time. Experimentation with design approaches to ensure that an implementation is feasible is also necessary. Many of the most effective developments are those in which there is a tight proactive iteration between detailed requirements, the design architecture to satisfy those requirements, and initial work to show that the resulting system will be adequately safe.

It is also important to note that the sequence of activities described above is not something carried out once. Safety analysis never ends. Hazard identification, the first main technical activity, is repeated a number of times during the life cycle (see Chapter 11).

2.3   HAZARD IDENTIFICATION AND RISK ASSESSMENT

As mentioned above, the process of identifying hazards is an early step in the process of controlling the risks to a tolerable level. This section expands on the hazard identification and risk assessment activities to show how they guide the level of rigour (via the safety integrity level) of the development, safety analysis and other activities, in order to mitigate the safety risks to an acceptable level. See Figure 2.1 for how they fit into the overall safety life cycle .

2.3.1   Overview of Safety Integrity

Section 2.1.1 showed that safety may be thought of in terms of freedom from unacceptable risk of harm. Risk may be defined as 'the combination of the frequency, or probability, of a hazard causing harm and the consequence if it did' [IEC 98]. The concept of risk thus has two parts, the probability of the occurrence of a harmful incident arising from a hazard and the consequences of that harmful incident.

Together with risk there is the concept of safety integrity, defined as 'the probability of a safety-related system satisfactorily performing the required safety functions under all the stated conditions within a stated period of time' [IEC 98].

Safety integrity has two components, random failure integrity and systematic failure integrity and both must be taken into consideration. Random failure integrity is generally closely related to the hardware reliability from random failures which can be predicted in a quantified manner to reasonable levels of confidence. However, it is much more difficult to estimate the frequency of systematic failures (those failures arising from human mistakes during the specification, design, construction, operation or maintenance of the system) because the failure rate depends on the inputs to the system and the state of the system when a particular set of inputs occurs. Systematic failures will always occur if the same conditions are repeated (however unlikely those conditions might be). All software failures are systematic failures but it is important to remember that systematic failure is also applicable to hardware logic, mechanical systems and incorrect installation or set up).

Emerging standards from the International Electrotechnical Committee [IEC 98] and the UK Ministry of Defence [MOD 95] use the concept of safety integrity level as the means of defining the required level of protection against systematic failure in the specification of the functions allocated to the safety-related systems. Appropriate design, development and safety analysis techniques are associated with each safety integrity level. The higher the integrity level the greater the degree of trust that is being placed in the system. This is expanded on below.

2.3.2   The Steps to Defining Safety Integrity Level

The IEC standard [IEC 98] gives a series of steps in the process of defining the safety integrity level and these are shown in Figure 2.5 and described below. An example of a computer-controlled instrument for delivering a drug to a patient via a hypodermic syringe in hospital operating theatres is used to illustrate each step. The assumption is made that the control system is produced under a good quality regime such as one which conforms to ISO 9000 [ISO 94].

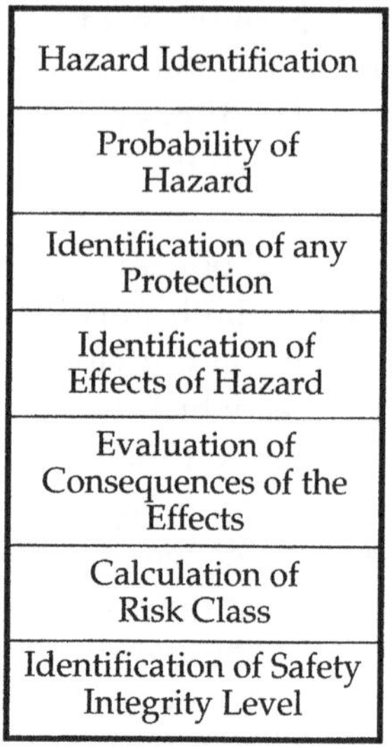

Hazard Identification
Probability of Hazard
Identification of any Protection
Identification of Effects of Hazard
Evaluation of Consequences of the Effects
Calculation of Risk Class
Identification of Safety Integrity Level

Figure 2.5: From hazard identification to integrity level

(a)   Hazard Identification

This is the process of identifying the hazardous situations that might result from things going wrong with a system or product. Techniques for hazard identification are described in the next section. For the drug delivery device a variety of things could go wrong that might result in the hazards of delivering more drug than the patient needs (over-delivery) and less drug than the patient needs (under-delivery). Examples of causes are an operator setting up the equipment with too high or too low a flow rate, and the control system malfunctioning and delivering more or less drug than is programmed by the operator.

Note that we use the word 'hazard' to describe both the system level hazards (the consequences) and the causes of those hazards. Above, we have identified the two hazards of over-delivery and under-delivery. These are the hazards that can be identified at the system level, without any knowledge of how the system is implemented. We then postulated causes of these hazards (such as user error or computer malfunction). Identifying those causes required knowledge of a basic decomposition of the system that both a user and a computer system are involved. At that increased level of knowledge, it is usual to speak of the causes of the system-level hazards as 'hazards' at that level. When yet more detail of the system is known, the causes of user error and computer malfunction may be identified and then, again, these will be referred to as 'hazards' at that increased level of detail.

(b)   Assign a Probability of Occurrence to Each of the Identified Hazards

Each identified cause of hazard has a qualitative probability of occurrence assigned to it. The qualitative probability classes that are often used, with meanings added for the example of the drug delivery system, are:

- Frequent, meaning likely to happen a number of times per operation;
- Probable, meaning likely to happen each operation;
- Occasional, meaning likely to happen a number of times in the life of one of the systems;
- Remote, meaning unlikely to happen during the life of one of the systems;
- Improbable, meaning may happen a number of times during the life of all instances of the system;
- Incredible, meaning highly unlikely to ever happen on any instance of the system.

For the example of the drug delivery system, hazards caused by user error may be deemed to be *probable,* those caused by a user taking positive hazardous action *occasional,* and those caused by errors in the computer system *occasional.*

(c)   Identify Mechanisms which Protect against Particular Hazards

This process takes each of the identified hazards, with its probability of occurrence, and identifies any protection that is in place against that hazard. In the drug delivery system, each protective device may, for example, be assumed to reduce the probability of occurrence by one step in the qualitative measure if it is effective and designed to a good quality regime such as ISO 9000. Thus a hazard 'user sets up delivery system wrongly' could have an estimated probability of *probable* but, because the computer control checks for this hazard, the assumed probability might be reduced to *occasional.* As an example, if an operator is asked to connect two parts of the system together, a simple protection mechanism would be for the computer system to check that there is electrical continuity between the two parts and not allow the set-up to continue until there is.

(d)   Identify Effects

This identifies the end (system-level) effect of each of the hazards. As mentioned above, this could be over-delivery or under-delivery. For one of the causes identified for the drug delivery device, the results of these four steps would be:

- Cause of hazard — user sets up delivery system wrongly;
- Probability of hazard — probable;
- Protection — computer controller;
- Probability of effect — occasional;
- Effect — over-delivery.

(e)   Identify Consequences of Effects

Four levels of consequence are often used. They, with interpretations, are as follows:

- Catastrophic, if it has the potential to result in multiple deaths or serious injuries;
- Critical, if it has the potential to result in a single death or serious injury;
- Marginal, if it has the potential to result in injury;
- Negligible, if it has little or no potential to result in injury.

Applying these to the example of the drug delivery device (and for a particular class of drug) we might say:

- A large over-delivery is critical — it could result in death or serious injury;
- A small over-delivery is negligible — it has little potential to result in injury;
- An under-delivery is negligible — it has little potential to result in injury.

For the system it may be reasonable to assume that over-delivery is usually small, but the possibility of large over-delivery must be taken into account. For the hazard identified, the critical consequence could be assumed to have an *occasional* probability of occurrence.

(f)   Calculate the Risk Class

A table may be used to assign a risk class from I to IV to each of the combinations of consequence and occurrence of risks — see Table 2.1, where

Table 2.1: A risk class matrix

	Negligible	*Marginal*	*Critical*	*Catastrophic*
Frequent	II	I	I	I
Probable	III	II	I	I
Occasional	III	III	II	I
Remote	IV	III	III	II
Improbable	IV	IV	III	III
Incredible	IV	IV	IV	IV

the probability of the hazard is given in the left hand column and the consequence of the effect is given along the top, with the remaining cells showing the assigned risk class. This is normally done for an industry sector, with due attention to a number of factors, including public opinion. In this table the risk level categories are identified as follows:

- Risk level I — intolerable risk;
- Risk level II — undesirable risk, tolerable only if reduction is impracticable or the costs are grossly disproportionate to the improvement gained;
- Risk class III — tolerable risk if the cost of risk reduction would exceed the improvement gained;
- Risk class IV — negligible risk.

The two middle risk classes (II and III) fit into the ALARP region introduced in the discussion of tolerability of risk in Section 2.1.1 and shown in Figure 2.2.

By carrying out the previous steps in the analysis of all identified hazards, a probability of occurrence is obtained for each of the possible consequences. For the example drug delivery device, in the previous step it was estimated that a certain *critical* consequence had an *occasional* probability of occurrence; putting that in the risk class table shows the associated risk to be in class II: undesirable.

(g) Identify the Safety Integrity Level

The final step in the process is to define a required safety integrity level for the safety-related systems which will be put in place to reduce the identified risks to tolerable levels. Until now we have assumed that the control system and its software have been developed under an ISO 9000 quality system and, in the example above, this results in a risk class of II: undesirable risk.

Unless it is impracticable to do so, the risk should be reduced to 'negligible', which is class IV, and this would be achieved by a safety-related system, the development of which would be carried out to the rigour demanded by a safety integrity level. The guidance in [IEC 98] suggests that the protection given by a development carried out to safety integrity level 1 may be claimed to reduce the risk class by 1 and a development to safety integrity level 4 may reduce the risk class by 3. In the example of the drug delivery device it is desirable to reduce the risk class by two steps from II to IV and so a development to integrity level 2 is needed.

2.4   HAZARD IDENTIFICATION TECHNIQUES

In the above sections we have moved from an overview of safety management systems, through the safety life cycle of systems and products, and examined the role of hazard identification and risk assessment in that life cycle. This section focuses on hazard identification (see the right-most column of Figure 2.1).

The section first gives an overview of some hazard identification techniques and then shows how two of the established techniques, hazard and operability studies (HAZOP) and fault modes and effects analysis (FMEA), take different approaches. To amplify the point that different techniques provide different viewpoints, the section then shows how two other safety analysis techniques, fault tree analysis (FTA) and event tree analysis (ETA), provide ways of examining, in a rigorous way, the causes and the consequences of the identified hazards.

2.4.1   Techniques for Hazard Identification

There are a variety of techniques used for identifying hazards in a system. Some of the most common will be described briefly. They are:

- What if?;
- Interaction matrix;
- Zonal analysis;
- Checklists;

- Fault modes and effects analysis (FMEA);
- HAZOP.

(a)   *What If?*

As the name implies, this asks a series of 'what if?' questions about the system and its design. Possible questions might be:

- What if
  - — a given mistake is made?
  - — equipment fails?
  - — a particular incident occurs?

The technique is useful to give a first assessment of hazards but is heavily reliant on the experience of those carrying out the review. Also, there is no assurance that the questions asked are sufficient in either breadth (coverage of the design, use and misuse of the system) or depth (the detail of the system or its use that is explored) to identify all the hazards.

(b)   *Interaction Analysis*

This looks at the interactions between specific aspects of a system. It is widely used in the process industries where chemicals could be mixed in error. The results are often given in the form of a matrix, with the constituent parts listed along each axis and the interactions occupying the cells. For a programmable system, possible interactions could be between a computer and electromagnetic interference (EMI) and two processes competing for a single resource.

(c)   *Zonal Analysis*

This also looks at interactions between components of a system, but is specifically concerned with their physical positions. It can be useful in identifying common cause hazards and the consequences of interconnection.

(d)   *Checklists*

Checklists help to identify hazards by providing a predetermined series of questions, usually related to 'what' and 'how'. They can be used to look at specific items of a system, or at procedures, and may be qualitative or quantitative. This approach can be used by a team or by a single person, at any time and at any level of design abstraction. The technique is reliant on the knowledge and experience of those producing the checklists and will normally require some subjective interpretation. Checklists can be useful in ensuring conformance with codes of practice and with standards and are most effective for systems where the design approach is already well understood. The major drawback is that the study will not look outside the checklist.

(e)   FMEA

This technique aims to identify the ways in which a system can fail and the effects of the failures. The steps in carrying out an FMEA are:

- Select a component;
- Identify its function;
- Select a fault mode;
- Identify the local effects (the effects of the fault on the immediately affected other components of the system);
- Identify system effects (the effects on the system as a whole);
- Identify methods of protection from the effects of the fault;
- Make recommendations.

An FMEA is normally carried out by an individual, but may be done by a team: it is one of the best known and most widely used systematic techniques for hazard identification. It can be very time-consuming if carried out for a whole system and has the drawbacks that it considers only single faults and does not address common-mode failures. More details of the use of FMEA may be found in *BS 5760 Part 5: Guide to Fault Mode and Effects and Criticality Analysis* [BSI 91a].

(f)   HAZOP

HAZOP is the application of a formal systematic technique to the identification of hazards. It examines the components and the interconnections between components so as to explore whether deviations from design intent are possible, and if so, what might be their causes and consequences. We have found that HAZOP is particularly powerful for exploring the interactions between parts of a system. HAZOP has a number of advantages:

- It is team based and brings a variety of viewpoints to the

identification;
- It is structured, thus ensuring thorough and consistent coverage;
- It can be used on operational systems as well as proposed designs;
- It can be carried out at all stages of a system's life;
- It is particularly effective for new systems or novel technologies.

2.4.2   How Techniques Complement Each Other

No one technique can claim to give complete identification of hazards and, in practice, a combination is likely to give the best results. The techniques of HAZOP and FMEA have different viewpoints and naturally complement each other, and it is a mistake to think of them as alternatives. Similarly, the techniques of fault tree analysis (FTA) and event tree analysis (ETA) complement each other in analysing the identified hazards in a highly structured way.

FMEA, often but erroneously referred to as failure mode and effects analysis, starts with a fault mode of a component and examines the effects of that fault. It thus works from the particular (a fault) to the general (all the effects of that fault) and so is an inductive technique. This is shown diagrammatically in Figure 2.6.

HAZOP starts with a particular deviation from design intent (say, a fault) and works both backwards to explore its possible causes and forwards to examine its consequences (as shown in Figure 2.7). The way in which HAZOP and FMEA complement each other is discussed in more detail in Chapter 11.

Once hazards have been identified, there is a need to assess the risks arising from them, as described in Sections 2.2 and 2.3.

FTA is a way of analysing system top-level hazards in terms of

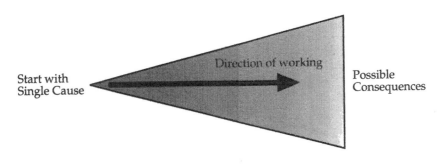

Start with
Single Cause

Direction of working

Possible
Consequences

Figure 2.6: FMEA — working forward from cause to possible consequences

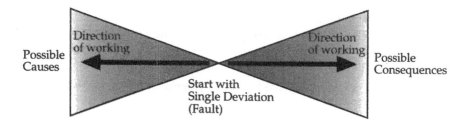

Figure 2.7: HAZOP — working from the fault both forwards to possible
consequences and backwards to possible causes

combinations of sub-system and lower-level events, and eventually down
to individual causes, such as component failures. The analysis is done in
simple steps breaking down the causes of the top-level failure by the use
of 'and' and 'or' gates so that a tree structure is produced. An 'and' gate is
used when the higher-level consequence can occur only as a result of a
combination of all the causes connected by the gate, and an 'or' gate when
any one of the causes could result in the higher-level consequence. FTA
thus moves backwards from the general (a top-level consequence or hazard)
to the particular (a set of low-level events) and so is a deductive technique
which needs a different tree to be generated for each top-level hazard. This
is shown diagrammatically in Figure 2.8. A detailed description of FTA
may be found in *BS 5760 Part 7: Guide to Fault Tree Analysis* [BSI 91b].

ETA is the natural complement to FTA. It also starts with a hazard but,
instead of working backwards to identify the causes as in FTA, it works
forwards to describe all the possible subsequent events and so identify the
event sequences which could lead to a variety of possible consequences.
From a diagrammatic point of view it is identical to Figure 2.6 for FMEA.

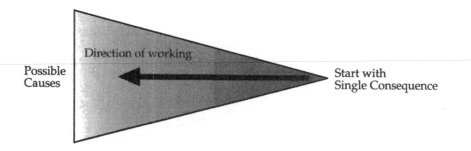

Figure 2.8: FTA — working back from consequence to causes

2.5 CONCLUDING REMARKS

In this chapter we have shown how the hazard identification technique, HAZOP, fits into the broad subject of managing safety.

- There is no such thing as absolute safety and the purpose of safety management activities is to reduce the risk of harm to an acceptable level.
- There is a well-accepted safety management circle, which includes the building of systems and products which will be adequately safe in use.
- A life cycle for systems and products is established which includes hazard identification and risk assessment as important parts. It is necessary to identify the hazards that might result from a particular activity or design and then assess the risks arising from those hazards before actions can be taken to reduce the risks to an acceptable level.
- There are a number of steps involved in identifying hazards, assessing risk and deciding on the risk reduction needed.
- Identifying the hazards is a vital first step and there are a variety of techniques available. Two of the more formal and established are HAZOP and FMEA. From examining the directions in which they work it is clear that the two can complement each other and should not be thought of as alternatives.

3
An Overview of HAZOP

A full description of HAZOP is developed over the course of this book, with each chapter being dedicated to the details of a particular aspect of it. To emerge with a clear understanding of the process, the reader needs to progress through the book. At the same time, in order to assimilate the concepts explained in the chapters, an understanding of their context is required, and this implies already having some familiarity with HAZOP. To overcome this 'catch 22' and to provide a context for the details offered in later chapters, this chapter provides an overview of the process and an introduction to the terms used.

3.1   INTRODUCTION

The purpose of HAZOP is to identify the hazards posed by a system so that, following their analysis, appropriate countermeasures may be taken to improve the safety of the system and its environment.

The central activity of a HAZOP is the investigation, by a team, of a description of the system under consideration — usually a representation of the design (the 'design representation'). In principle there is no restriction on the form that the design representation can take, as long as it is clearly documented and understood by all the team members (see Chapter 4). For example, for a chemical plant it may be a piping and instrumentation diagram (P&ID), for an electrical system a circuit diagram, for an electronic control system a data flow diagram, and if the order of events is relevant, a state transition diagram. Included in the design representation, or appended to it, there may be operational instructions or other information.

The investigation progresses methodically, under the control of a study leader, and typically extends over a number of meetings. It must be planned and the results must be recorded. For convenience of understanding, it is described in this chapter as a four-staged process. However, each of these stages in fact consists of a number of functions, and these will be described individually in subsequent chapters. The four sequential stages are:

- Initiating the study (see Chapter 5);
- Planning the study (see Chapters 6, 7 and 8);
- Holding the study meetings (see Chapter 9);
- Dealing with follow-up work (see Chapter 10).

Whereas the significance of the technical aspects of HAZOP should not be minimised, HAZOP is a team activity and depends for its success on the interactions of the team members. It is therefore crucial that the team is optimally composed, and that the team leader is capable of leadership and of controlling the process. The skills of the team members should be complementary and the members themselves should between them possess the appropriate abilities for contributing effectively to the team effort. Whether team interaction is harmonious, efficient and effective then depends largely on the leadership and control of the study leader. The influence and importance of human factors on the process cannot be over-emphasised

HAZOP may be carried out on a system at any stage of its life cycle — at the conceptual stage, when the system is under development, or after it has become operational. The need for HAZOP during a development project should be identified at the commencement of the project and defined in the project safety plans; similarly, the timing of HAZOPs during the operational life should be defined in the system's operation plans.

3.2 INITIATING THE STUDY

If a HAZOP is to be carried out successfully, it needs to be planned in advance and someone in the organisation needs to be made responsible for it. In the first instance, the need for HAZOP studies, and their timing, should be defined in both project and operational plans. Then, the responsibility for the studies should be invested in a named person — the 'study initiator', who may be a safety manager or some other manager with appropriate authority. The study initiator should possess:

- An understanding of HAZOP and its advantages and limitations;
- Knowledge of when a study is necessary;
- A well defined responsibility for ensuring that the study is planned and carried out successfully;
- The authority to initiate the study;
- Sufficient understanding of the project or operational system to ensure that the study is planned effectively;
- The authority to provide support to the study if this is necessary for making it effective or efficient.

When a HAZOP is appropriate, the study initiator should define the scope and objectives of the study, appoint a suitable study leader, and brief the study leader on the scope of the study and what is expected from it. If necessary, he should also arrange for the study leader to have discussion meetings with appropriate persons (such as the system owner and the system designer) in order to familiarise himself with the overall purpose of the system and with the design representation(s) of the system (see Sections 3.3 and 3.4) to be used as the basis of the study.

The study initiator should then be available to assist the study leader in planning the HAZOP and should monitor the study and be ready with support in the event of difficulties or uncertainties. More detailed advice on the responsibilities of the study initiator is offered in Chapter 5.

3.3   PLANNING THE STUDY

A HAZOP can be a lengthy process and usually extends over a number of meetings. The study leader should plan the study (see Chapters 6, 7 and 8 for details of what this involves), with assistance, as necessary, from the study initiator. The main planning considerations are:

- Ensuring the availability of an appropriate design representation (see Chapter 4).
- Selecting the study team members and ensuring their availability (see Chapter 6).
- Identifying the properties of the design representation to be examined during the study. These are based on the system components and

the interconnections between them, as depicted on the design representation, and are the 'entities' and 'attributes' described in Chapter 4.

- Determining how many study meetings will be necessary, scheduling them, and arranging their accommodation and other logistic necessities.
- Selecting the 'guide words' for use in the study and determining the interpretations of the guide words when they are applied to the particular attributes on the design representation (see Chapter 7). A 'guide word' is a word or phrase which expresses and defines a specific type of 'deviation from design intent'. An example is 'more' which guides the study to consider whether it is feasible for there to be more of the attribute under study. A generic list of guide words is given in Section 7.1 of Chapter 7. When the study leader is not expert in the design representation under consideration, guide-word selection and interpretation should be done in collaboration with a design expert.
- Briefing the study team members.

3.4   HOLDING THE STUDY MEETINGS

The study leader 'chairs' study meetings and is responsible for ensuring that they are effective (see Chapter 9). An outline of the process of a HAZOP meeting is given in Figure 3.1.

At the start of the first meeting, the study leader introduces the team members, reviews the plans which have been sent to them to remind them of what is to be done and how it is to be done, and ensures that everyone is familiar with the HAZOP process. He or she then invites the designer to present the design representation and confirm that the team members understand both the system and the particular type of representation to be studied.

Following these introductions, the study leader commences the examination of the design representation. The purpose of this is to identify hazards and their causes and consequences, in accordance with the defined scope and objectives of the study. The method is to investigate what deviations could occur in the values of the attributes of entities from their 'design intent', what effects the deviations could have, and what could cause them. This is done by a step-by-step process under the control of the study leader.

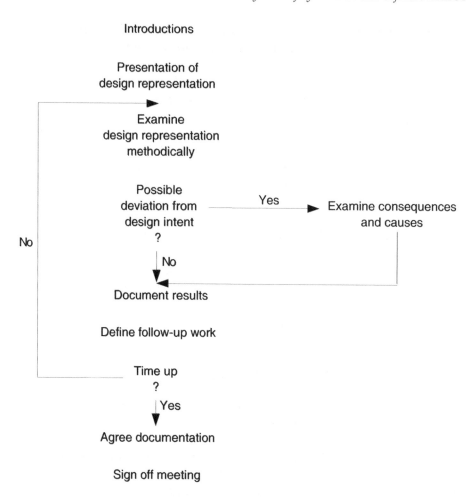

Figure 3.1: An outline of the process of a HAZOP meeting

First the study leader selects an entity on the design representation. The entity may be a component of the design (such as a processor) or an interconnection between two components (such as a data stream). The choice of this first entity should be according to a predetermined pattern and should normally be at an appropriate logical position on the design representation (such as the input, if progress is to be from input to output, or the output, if progress is to be in the reverse direction).

The next step is to select an attribute, or property, of the entity, for it is the attributes which are given design values from which there may be deviation. Considering as an example a control signal used to trigger the closure of the plant in an emergency, such a signal must have a specific value or it would not be interpreted correctly, with the result that the plant would not be shut down (or that it might be shut down incorrectly). In this case, the 'value' of the stream of data which composes the signal is an attribute of the data.

The identification of deviations is based on the use of predetermined 'guide words', each of which focuses attention on a particular type of possible deviation. As a guide word is applied to the attribute under investigation, the question which the guide word raises is asked. An example of a guide word is 'more', and it raises the questions, 'What would happen if there was more of the attribute?' and 'Could there be more of the attribute, and if so how?' The answers to these questions lead to an understanding of whether the defined deviation from design intent could occur and if so how and with what consequences. In the above example, the guide word 'more' would be interpreted as 'greater', giving rise to the question: 'What would happen if the value of the control signal were greater than it should be?' And if the answer were, 'The plant would not be shut down', this would be an indication of a hazard.

As a guide word may have different interpretations depending on the circumstances (in the example above 'more' was interpreted as 'greater'), not only the guide words but also their interpretations in the given context are important. Thus, the study employs a number of attribute-guide-word-interpretations, the selection of which is an important part of the planning (see Chapter 7 for details). As each combination is applied, the focus of the team is guided to a particular type of deviation to examine whether it is meaningful with respect to that attribute of that particular entity. If the answer is yes, the team enquires into the possible causes and consequences of the deviation. In this way, hazardous (and other) consequences are identified.

When the guide words chosen for use in the study have all been applied to the first attribute, the other attributes of the entity under consideration are examined in turn. When all attributes of an entity have been studied, the study leader marks off the entity as having been studied and selects the next in the logical progression across the design representation. The process is then repeated for each entity on the design representation.

The process is continued, possibly over several meetings, until the entire design representation has been subjected to a systematic investigation. At each meeting the results are recorded according to a predetermined procedure (see Chapter 10). The main results are the hazards discovered, their causes, consequences, and any conclusions drawn about them, recommendations for follow-up work, and questions which could not be answered at the meeting but which need to be resolved in order for a given aspect of the study to be completed at a subsequent meeting. The follow-up work usually relates to uncertainties which must be resolved before the study can be concluded.

Redesign of the system is not within the ambit of a HAZOP study, and the team should not concern itself with this. Yet, if the necessary mitigation of a hazard is obvious to the team it would be silly not to capture it in the recommendations, particularly if the relevant experts happen to be present at the study. At the same time, the effectiveness of the study depends on using the time available for hazard identification, and extraneous discussion should be minimised.

A study meeting ends with the documentation of the activities of the study. All documentation should be agreed by the team and signed off by the study leader. A HAZOP ends when the design representation has been studied in its entirety (over the course of a series of meetings) and all questions raised during the process have been resolved.

3.5   DEALING WITH FOLLOW-UP WORK

If there are uncertainties at a HAZOP meeting which are relevant to the understanding of the discovered hazards, their causes, or their consequences, or which may have led to hazards not being discovered, the study cannot be concluded until they have been answered and the associated issues resolved at a subsequent meeting. In other words, a HAZOP must end on conclusions and recommendations and not questions. Questions may refer to any of a number of issues, examples being the details of the design representation, the meaningfulness of deviations, the possible causes and consequences of deviations, and the effectiveness of any existing or proposed protection or mitigation systems or components.

The resolution of questions between study meetings is often necessary (and is a part of a study meeting's 'follow-up work'). When relevant follow-up work has been carried out, the results may need to be fed into a subsequent meeting in the same study. Typically, as questions are raised at consecutive meetings, they and their resolutions are 'batched' and related issues are resolved 'en masse'.

When questions are raised at a meeting near the end of the planned study schedule, it may be necessary to add one or more meetings to the end of the schedule in order to deal with the results of follow-up work and complete the thorough examination of the design representation. This may also be necessary if an unusually large number of questions are raised during the course of the study. However, in some cases it may not be possible to answer all questions before the HAZOP team is disbanded. Then, each outstanding question should be converted into a recommendation for further study and resolution by a certain defined point in the development or use, as appropriate in the circumstances, of the system under study.

3.6   CONCLUDING REMARKS

This chapter has provided a brief overview of HAZOP, intended to provide the reader with sufficient background to understand the content of the subsequent chapters and the terms used in them. The reader wishing to learn the process should now study Chapters 4 to 10 in order.

4

Representations and Attributes

As introduced in Chapters 1 and 3, the key feature of HAZOP is the structured study of representations of the system design. A wide variety of design representations are in use, and almost any can be the basis of a HAZOP.

When HAZOP is applied in the chemical industry, the word 'parameter' is often used to describe the 'features' of the design, for example temperature, pressure, and rate of flow of the chemicals in the plant. In this book, we use the word 'attribute' instead of 'feature' or 'parameter'.

This chapter first discusses design representations that have been used successfully for HAZOP, and how to use them. It then considers how achieving a complete study depends on identifying the design attributes covered by the representations and checking them for completeness.

4.1   REPRESENTATIONS

A representation portrays the intention of the designer through the features of the design. The representation can take many forms and may be more or less detailed, depending on the stage in the design process that the development has reached. It is often pictorial, but it does not have to be, and other forms have been used successfully. Generally, representations use symbols, text, or a mixture of the two to show the design intent. Often it is not possible to contain the complete representation on a single sheet of paper, so multiple sheets will be used. The HAZOP team will then study each sheet in turn.

The design representation may be either physical or logical. Physical representations show the physical 'real world' layout of the system and are useful for determining hazards that might be caused by a system's physical layout or whose consequences might be made worse by it. For example, one piece of moving equipment might be able to strike another piece and thus cause an accident. In a chemical plant with flammable materials, a fire from a small leak might heat another pipe that is above the initial leak and cause a larger release of flammable substances. Such hazards will be found only if the physical representation is studied.

Logical representations show the logical relationships between the components and are useful for determining hazards due to them. For example, a hazard might exist because one element of a system can pass incorrect data to another element, which then acts on it. It is their logical relationship that causes the hazard; physically they could be millimetres or kilometres apart. Most HAZOP studies use logical representations of systems as the basis for the early studies and then move on to study the physical representations at a later stage.

In many systems, both physical and logical representations will need to be examined in at least one of the hazard identification studies carried out during the system life cycle. This is because both may impact on the hazards and their causes. If the two items of equipment mentioned above were two computer systems in the same control room, each with its own operator, the operators might be able to communicate rapidly and thus control the hazard. However, if they were in separate control rooms, such communication might be more difficult and an accident might not be averted. If we fail to examine both types of representation, either we might not detect a hazard or the study team might consider a hazard to be less important than it is and thus not draw it to the designer's attention so strongly.

We believe that almost any representation can be used during a HAZOP, but we also believe that some are better than others, as discussed below. The only restrictions that we would place on which representations should be used are that they must in some form or another capture the intent of the designer, and the HAZOP team must understand them.

4.1.1   Good Representations are Essential to the Success of a HAZOP

The representations of the design of the system to be studied are a critical aspect of any HAZOP. Without suitable ones, the process is not a HAZOP and without good ones the study may fail or be less successful.

The best representations are those that enable the HAZOP team easily and rapidly to understand the design intent and then to identify and explore all the critical attributes of the system. If the team cannot easily understand the intent, they will spend a lot of time discussing the design and not identifying hazards. This is further discussed below in Section 4.1.2.

When using HAZOP we have found few problems on representations that enabled us correctly to identify the components, interactions, attributes, guide words and interpretations that needed to be studied (see Section 4.2 and Chapter 7 for a further explanation of these aspects of HAZOP). When representations do not facilitate this, the HAZOP team can easily become immersed in discussion about what they are studying, and this may reduce the efficiency of the study or cause them to fail to identify items that need to be studied. When, because of the limitations of the representations used, such identification is not possible, the study will be incomplete. The team will not perform a truly systematic study, as it will only examine a subset of the relevant components, interactions, attributes, guide words and interpretations. As a result it may not find all the hazards posed by the system. So a good representation must enable the team to identify the elements of the system that they need to study.

The representation is also a key means of control used by the study leader in running the HAZOP sessions. The representation acts as an 'agenda' for the team, as it tells them the elements they must study. In a representation where the elements for study are not clear, the team will lack this agenda. This means that they might fail to study an element of importance. In our experience the team will often be less productive since, just as in any meeting with no agenda, they will tend to wander and it will be much more difficult for the study leader to control them. In preparing the representations, the study leader should ensure that they completely cover the defined scope of the study and will serve as a useful agenda. This is further discussed in Section 4.1.3.

Most HAZOP studies are carried out with pictorial representations of the design. There are, however, times when one type of pictorial representation is more appropriate than another. For example, at an early stage of the development life cycle, when overall system hazards are being identified, a simple block diagram may be most appropriate, but later when timing is studied a timing diagram is desirable.

Each type of representation has its own set of methods used to portray the features of the design, and the symbols used have predefined meanings. Thus, there is a certain type of information that each representation presents. For example, a block diagram expresses the logical relationships between components and a data flow diagram expresses the flows of information between components of a computer-based system. Neither explicitly shows attributes such as 'timing', 'bit rate' or 'sequence' but, in some cases, these may be inferred. If the study is to be complete, the representations used should cover those aspects of a system that could, if they do not achieve the design intent, cause hazards. If a single design representation does not, or cannot, cover all the attributes or credible failures relevant to the study, then one or more other types of representation will be required. Unless the design or other very similar designs have already been studied in detail, it must be assumed that all parts of the system could cause a hazard, so we must aim to have a representation that shows the complete design, within the scope of the study.

Before commencing the study, the attributes presented should be reviewed so as to check that an adequate representation is available (see Section 4.2). If any are missing from the representation, as discussed in Section 4.2.2, further representations should be identified, otherwise the study will be incomplete (see Chapter 8 for further information about planning the study).

4.1.2   The Study Team must Understand the Representations

It is important that all the members of the HAZOP team understand the design representations. In practice this can be a constraint on the choice of team members, but the lack of understanding of team members should never be a constraint on the selection of the representations. Our experience is that while, for example, data flow diagrams and system block diagrams are easy for the non-expert to understand with a little extra training, some representations, such as chemical process piping and instrumentation diagrams (P&IDs) and functional programming languages, require more knowledgeable team members. A lack of knowledge will impair the HAZOP process, unless more extensive training is carried out.

The use of a P&ID as the main representation of chemical plant in HAZOPs has been an important factor in achieving successful studies. A

P&ID is a logical representation of the plant. It enables the team to 'follow' the chemical processes from start to finish, and rapidly understand the way in which the plant functions. With some extra information, for example on vessel design and operating instructions, it is possible to study the hazards of the plant design. However, hazards due to physical aspects of the design, for example the positions of pumps and pipe racks, will have to be studied by the use of another representation unless a knowledgeable HAZOP leader can ensure that the correct questions are asked during the HAZOP. This review of the physical aspects might include a plant inspection of areas about which concerns have been raised.

When we deliberately conducted experimental HAZOP trials on representations that the study leader did not understand in detail, we found that the lack of understanding significantly impaired the HAZOP process. It was only when the study leader had learnt more about the representations that the HAZOP was successful. It is clear from these trials that the study leader must have a full understanding of the representations. This is not to say that the study leader has to be an expert on the system under study, just that he or she must fully understand the selected representation. When other team members did not fully understand the representations this had a lesser effect on the trial study, but still proved to be important. It is, therefore, necessary for all team members to receive sufficient training to enable them to understand the representations used in a given study. In our experience, this need not be too time-consuming, with a half hour exercise often being sufficient for some pictorial representations. However, half a day was required for a functional programming language. The time spent training all the team members so that they can contribute effectively to the hazard identification is never wasted.

One particularly important member of the HAZOP team is the system user who may have little, if any, knowledge of the design representations being used. However, the user is often someone who possesses significant practical operational experience and needs to be included in the HAZOP team. For example, a pilot, or even an aeronautical engineer, is unlikely to understand a formal mathematical language used as the design representation of a high-integrity avionics system. This may present special problems, and the need for extra training or preparation must be taken into account in planning the study.

One approach that has been suggested to overcome the problem of lack of knowledge of the design representation is to create a pictorial representation specifically for use in HAZOP. We do not recommend this, because doing so can introduce misrepresentations of the designer's intent.

This can result in certain deviations not being studied, as they may appear to be intended. Translation to a new representation is also subject to errors, which may again mask hazards.

Despite these pitfalls, there are some cases where the study requires that a representation be developed — for example, when none exists or when the existing one does not cover the complete system with all its interfaces (a rather common problem). Chapter 13 discusses how to do this when the system includes significant human interaction. In this context we have often developed hierarchical task analysis representations of projects, such as the relocation of a control room. When this means that some form of translation of or addition to an existing design representation is needed, care must be taken. Further, when it is deemed necessary to develop a representation for use in a HAZOP, this needs to be done at the planning stage of the HAZOP, as described in Section 8.2. It must also be recorded and the representations developed included in the HAZOP report.

4.1.3   The Representations must Cover all Aspects of the System being Studied

A HAZOP must use representations that embrace all the elements of the system which fall within the defined scope of the study. However, on occasions we have been asked to study a representation that does not include critical elements of the system. In some of these cases the missing elements included critical items such as the utilities of the chemical plant (air, nitrogen, etc.) or the system's operator. As a result the study was deemed to be incomplete. The study leader must always ensure the representations used cover the full scope of the HAZOP, and that, if they extend beyond the scope of the study, the scope is clearly marked on them.

When selecting the representations to be used in a HAZOP, the study leader must ensure that they cover all the attributes of the system that could affect the system's safety. If they do not, the HAZOP must be clearly identified as a partial study. This is discussed in more detail in Section 4.2, as it is also the completeness of the attributes that will determine the completeness of the representations. It is necessary, when selecting the representations, to check that they cover all the physical and logical aspects of the system that could cause a hazard. If logical representations are to be used, but the physical layout or timing are important aspects of the safety of the system, then it must be accepted that logical representations are not a complete representation of the system in the context of safety.

4.1.4   The Problems of Multiple Representations

If a single type of representation does not cover all the aspects of the system that the team wish to study, two or more representations must be used. It must be clearly identified which aspects are to be studied on each one.

When multiple representations are used, normal practice is for the team to study each representation in turn, in a sequential manner. This can present a number of problems that need to be managed during the HAZOP.

Firstly, certain points may be noted or raised by the team on one representation that are better studied on another. Secondly, the possible deviations from design intent raised as credible on one representation will need to be properly taken into account on the other representations when they are studied. Thirdly, when the team members start on a new representation, there is a tendency for them to say: 'We have already studied it. Let's just add a note saying "see previous representation"'. However, as a deviation may have causes or consequences that are apparent only on the new representation, this must be avoided.

When multiple representations are studied, we strongly suggest that the study leader uses a formal system, with rules and documentation of the study's adherence to the rules, to track the points raised by the team. The study leader must be particularly aware of the need to avoid the 'we have already studied that' syndrome. Section 12.2 in Chapter 12 gives detailed guidance on this problem.

Using multiple representations in parallel (which has been suggested as a solution to the above concerns) can be potentially confusing. This is because team members will have to retain their understanding of all of the representations at the same time. If, however, there are multiple representations that can be studied in parallel without creating confusion among the team, we recommend that this be done. One example is where they show the same components and interactions in a consistent and traceable manner. A trial prior to the HAZOP will soon show whether this approach will work with any given set of representations. If any confusion arises during the trial, we recommend that the representations be studied separately. A good example of where this approach works well is during a chemical plant HAZOP which uses the P&ID representation as the basic guide for the study but also uses other representations, such as operations and maintenance manuals and plot plans, when needed.

4.1.5 Compound Flows need to be Managed Carefully

Some HAZOP teams have experienced difficulty with compound interconnections between components on a design. This often arises on representations of chemical plants when two or more chemicals flow in the same pipe and on representations of computer-based systems, such as data flow diagrams, where the flow on an interconnection may be anything from a single data item to a group of any number of items.

On a high-level diagram, a single interconnection may be descriptive of the whole group. Decomposition into subgroups and then into primitive single item flows takes place on successively more detailed design representations. Ultimately, it is the primitive single item flows that need to be studied at some time during one of the HAZOP studies conducted. If only one HAZOP is carried out, the individual flows must be identified and addressed in that study. In other cases, when a hierarchical decomposition is available, it is usual to consider the primitive flows when the decomposition reaches the appropriate level. Further information on this problem, and how to address it, is given in Chapter 12.

4.1.6 Typical Representations and their Use in HAZOP

Examples of representations on which we have conducted HAZOPs include:

- Piping and instrumentation diagrams (P&IDs) (see [CIA 77] for simple examples);
- Block diagrams of the system (electrical, mechanical and pneumatic);
- Detailed electrical schematics;
- Detailed mechanical drawings;
- Detailed pneumatic schematics;
- Data flow diagrams, including those of human activities (see Chapters 7 and 13 for further information);
- State transition diagrams (see Sections 7.4.2 and 15.1 for further information);
- Object orientated design diagrams (see Sections 7.4.4 and 15.2 for further information);
- Functional programming languages;
- Timing diagrams;
- Operating instructions;
- Procedures;
- Hierarchical task analyses (HTAs) [Annett 71; Kirwan 92];

• Circuit diagrams.

Of the above representations, we have found that functional programming languages and state transition diagrams have presented the most significant initial problems. This is because they present the greatest difficulty to the identification of the attributes of the design. It is also difficult to develop clear definitions of the interpretations of the deviations from design intent. Given these two problems, we have found that most teams studying these representations require a substantial amount of time to become accustomed to the HAZOP process on them. It is therefore essential that the attributes, guide words and interpretations are clearly defined prior to the study of these difficult representations. We also recommend that the team start the study with a detailed review of the method used to portray the features of the design in these representations. This should be followed by a prolonged trial study (we would suggest 3 hours). If this preparation and trial are carried out, such representations can be studied effectively using the HAZOP technique.

Hierarchical task analyses (HTAs) show how tasks are achieved, by breaking them down into a hierarchy of more detailed tasks. HTAs are often difficult to use, as they do not always capture all the attributes of the design. One example is when the tasks involve data flows and interactions between the people carrying out complex data-intensive or non-sequential activities (i.e. where activities may occur in parallel with no sequencing between them, but with important interactions). An HTA study on its own is more suited to an FMEA-based approach (see Chapter 11 for a comparison of FMEA and HAZOP). If HAZOP is used, then other representations are required to study the interaction, timing and data flow hazards. HAZOP can be used, if desired, where the HTA is of a truly sequential series of tasks which are not data-intensive and which have no significant non-sequential information flows.

Mechanical drawings are not normally used during a HAZOP. However, if the design components and interactions can be identified, they can be used. This is especially true if there is some degree of design abstraction involved. If they contain significant design detail, FMEA may be a more suitable technique (again, see Chapter 11).

We have successfully used data flow representations for HAZOPs of operating instructions, procedures and human-machine interactions (see Chapter 13 for some examples). We recognise that these aspects may not always be captured by an existing representation, so the study may require that a new design representation (for example, a data flow diagram) be developed, as discussed in Section 4.1.2.

4.2 ATTRIBUTES

In this book we have called both the design components and the interactions between them 'entities'. All entities have design features that need to be studied during a HAZOP. On a design representation, a path between two components indicates an interaction between the components. An interaction consists of a transfer, or flow, from one component to another. A flow may be tangible (such as a chemical compound) or intangible (such as an item of data). In either case the flow is designed with certain properties, which we have called 'attributes'. These affect how the system functions and perhaps the safety of the system. Examples of attributes are the 'temperature' of a chemical and the 'speed' of its flow.

In a similar way the components of the system will also have attributes, which reflect the way in which they function. A data store, for example, would have attributes such as how full it is, and the speed of storage and retrieval.

The correct operation of the system is determined by the attributes of the interactions and components keeping to their design values (the 'design intent'). It follows that by studying what would happen if the attributes deviate from design intent, we should identify the hazards of the system. This is the principle of HAZOP. It is therefore necessary that the attributes shown on a representation or set of representations provide a clear and complete description of how the system functions. If attributes exist which could affect the safety of the system when they deviate from design intent, but which are not included in the representations being used, then the hazards which could arise from them will be missed. It is vital that the representations used include all such attributes. In fact, it is the key criterion in determining whether the set of representations is sufficient for the HAZOP study.

4.2.1 Attributes Depend on the Design Representations

The attributes available for the study will depend on the representations used. An interconnection or component shown on a design represents one or more attributes, either explicitly or implicitly. In a P&ID the attributes 'temperature', 'pressure' and 'flow' are not represented explicitly, but are implicit in each pipe shown. Within the chemical industry they are always considered in a HAZOP even though they are not explicit. In a similar way on a data flow diagram, the attribute of 'data rate' is not directly shown on each data interconnection, but it is easy for the HAZOP team to recognise it as being an attribute of the data flow. The study leader must therefore identify the implicit and explicit attributes in advance of the study and make the implicit ones clear. This can be done either by writing them on the representation or by creating a list which is then given to each team member.

Each design representation includes certain attributes of the design, but most do not contain all the attributes that could contribute to hazards. When preparing for HAZOP two questions require to be addressed:

- What attributes are covered by the representations being used?
- Are the attributes covered sufficient for identifying the possible hazards?

This process is described in more detail below.

4.2.2   Checking the Attributes during HAZOP Preparation

Ensuring that all relevant attributes are addressed requires a two-staged process. First, every entity should be defined and all its attributes (explicit or implicit) identified on each representation. This process will require the study leader to examine the representations, possibly with the help of the designer or other study leaders with experience of the particular type of representation. The study leader should then identify each entity of the design and the way it is represented. Once this is done, the attributes of the entities (whether they are explicitly or implicitly represented) should be identified, again possibly through discussion with the designer or another study leader. An example of this for a P&ID representation is to consider the interconnection entity 'a pipe' and then its attributes 'flow', 'pressure', 'temperature', etc.

Second, the attributes identified should be checked for completeness. This check consists of a further review of all the entities on the design representations. Attribute lists from other studies should be employed, with each checked against the entities on the representations. This is to verify that no other attributes exist which could have an impact on safety.

Another useful check is to develop two lists, one of all the entities and one of all the attributes. By comparing these two lists, a check is carried out for any possible entity-attribute combination not previously identified. Thus, for example, if the two lists contain 'pump' and 'electric current', and the study leader had failed to identify 'electric current' as an attribute of 'pump' but the current drawn by the pump could be significant, a way of considering it must be found, either on the existing representation or on a new one.

The study leader should also consider what other attributes might be of importance and ensure that they are considered. For example, the attribute 'temperature' is not represented on a data flow diagram, but if it is known to be an important factor in the safety of the system under study, completeness can be achieved only if a further representation is employed. Another example follows on from the discussion of HTA given above. If the study leader feels that the attributes of the data flowing between the people carrying out the tasks (such as 'data rate', 'data value', 'flow', etc.) are important but not represented, then another representation should be used.

The final result of this checking process should be a final list of entity-attribute relationships that will be studied during the HAZOP. It may be useful to review this list with the system's designers prior to the HAZOP and present it to the HAZOP team before commencing the study.

While it is crucial to ensure completeness, we are not aware of any technique that can guarantee it. We have found that the combination of systematic review, a cross-check of separate entity and attribute lists prior to the study, the use of the results of previous studies, and the experience of the study leader, all help to ensure that the HAZOP is as complete as possible. A good study leader will also be attentive to new attributes that might be noted during the study and will take appropriate action in respect of them. This will include a review of all the previous sections of the HAZOP, to ascertain the effect of including the new attribute, and the inclusion of the new attribute in the remaining HAZOP study meetings.

Typical attributes for some design representations are given in Chapters 7, 13 and 15.

4.3   CONCLUDING REMARKS

This chapter has described two of the key aspects of the HAZOP process, namely the design representations and the attributes they present. It offers guidance on the selection of representations. It also discusses where multiple representations may be needed and the problems that these can cause. Attributes and entities are explained, as are some techniques for ensuring that as complete a set of attributes as possible is available.

5
The Study Initiator's Role in HAZOP

In order to provide confidence that a HAZOP will be carried out efficiently, effectively, and at the appropriate time, it should be the responsibility of a named 'study initiator'. The purpose of this chapter is to explain the process of HAZOP initiation and define the role of the study initiator.

5.1   INTRODUCTION

Before a system is brought into operation, and then if changes are made to it or its environment during operation, it is necessary to gain assurance that it is safe. The importance of carrying out safety analyses and applying techniques such as HAZOP is therefore apparent. Indeed, notwithstanding such a merely rational view, there may be more precisely defined reasons why hazard analyses are necessary, for example:

- It may be company policy that all systems, or parts of systems, should be subjected to certain analyses, either before being released from development or before being brought into operation;
- The customer may have specified a requirement for particular

analyses to be carried out;
- There is often a need to satisfy regulatory requirements for safety;
- For safety-critical systems, doing everything practicable to identify and mitigate hazards may be a legal necessity, because the developers and operators are potentially liable should breaches of safety occur;
- It is necessary to identify the hazards posed by a system before a safety integrity level (SIL) can be defined for the system;
- Safety-related incidents can result in financial loss.

In spite of the many good reasons to identify the hazards posed by a system, it is not uncommon for the need for HAZOP to be neglected by someone engrossed in the day-to-day management of system development or operation. Time pressure, budget and technical problems, and the need to satisfy conflicting demands on limited resources, frequently lead to the neglect of certain tasks which are not perceived as essential to the job in hand. Project and operational managers may not see HAZOP as crucial to the achievement of their own immediate goals, and many are not acquainted with hazard and safety analysis and not aware of their importance to achieving safety. Perhaps they should be, but often they are not. In any case, the 'right thing' does not happen by chance.

But if the right thing does not happen by chance, a system should be put in place to ensure that it happens. Where safety is concerned, the reasons mentioned in the previous paragraph for not taking appropriate action do not form a legal defence. Where harm occurs, individuals, and in particular the more senior individuals, may be subject to criminal proceedings. Under certain legislation, the senior manager has direct responsibility for doing all that is practicable to ensure safety, and he or she should be supported by an active management system which itself is managed and made to work. Within such a system, initiating a HAZOP should be the responsibility of someone other than those involved in the day-to-day development or operation of the system. The 'study initiator' may be a senior manager with overall responsibility for the development project or operational system, a safety officer in the organisation developing or operating it, or some other person of authority. He or she should have the responsibility for initiating and monitoring the study and for providing support whenever it is needed in order for the study to meet its objectives.

5.2   PROJECT PLANS

The safety analysis activities can and should be defined at the outset of a project or at the start of the operational life of a system, and they should be shown within the project or operational plans. The study initiator's identity and the extent of his responsibility and authority should also be included in the plans so that the project or operational manager knows not only when studies are to be carried out but also whom to liaise with over the readiness (or lateness) of the appropriate parts of the system for study. Identifying the study initiator in the project plans carries the additional advantage that it is clear (to the study initiator) that neglect of the responsibility would not go unnoticed. In other words, a procedure is created with built-in checks on all parties.

In the case of a development project, the study initiator should have a continuing interest in the project, should be familiar with the project plans, and should be aware of the progress of the project. (It may be noted that the project manager is not precluded from being the study initiator.) In the case of an operational system, the study initiator should keep aware of the use and history of the system — its quality of service, breakdown rate, accident rate, safety record, etc.

There may be exceptional occasions when unplanned HAZOPs are necessary, for example when there has been a significant change to the requirements on the system or to the system's intended environment, either during a development project or during operation. Allowance should be made for this, and the person or persons responsible for reviewing the safety plans under such conditions should be identified. Their responsibility to liaise with the study initiator, to ensure that the extra study is appropriately initiated and supported, should be defined. (The duties of the study initiator are given in the following sections.)

5.3   SELECTING THE STUDY LEADER

Having ensured that the HAZOPs to be carried out on a given system are defined in the project or operational plans, the study initiator needs to liaise with the manager in charge (for example, the project or operations manager) at the appropriate times and confirm the decisions to carry out the studies.

Once it is confirmed that a given study will be carried out, the study initiator needs first to define the scope and objectives of the study (see

Section 5.4) and then to appoint a study leader. As will be seen in Chapter 6, a study leader must have certain qualifications, so the task is not simply that of finding someone willing to do the job. A person suitable to lead a study on the particular type of system in question must be chosen. In principle, the study initiator is not precluded from being the study leader.

The study leader need not have prior familiarity with the particular system to be studied; indeed, a degree of independence is often an advantage, as an important aspect of the study leader's role is to avoid discussion of the details of the system and concentrate the study on identifying hazards. However, in order to lead an effective study, the study leader requires an adequate understanding of the principles of the system under study and of the design representations to be studied.

The study initiator needs to brief the study leader, providing an outline of the system and what is required of the study. The study initiator must ensure that the study leader receives copies of the design representations and that he is conversant with them. It may be useful for the study initiator to hold a meeting with the study leader and one of the system's designers to discuss the system, its purpose and its overall design, and the particular conventions employed on the design representation to be used in the HAZOP. In the case of an operational system, the study leader may need to meet the operational manager so as to be acquainted with the system's modes of operation and operating environment, and he or she may also want to see the system in operation.

5.4   SCOPE AND OBJECTIVES OF THE STUDY

If the effort invested in a HAZOP is to be efficiently and effectively employed, the terms of reference, in the form of the study's scope and objectives, must be clearly defined by the study initiator and then adhered to by the study leader in conducting the study.

5.4.1   Scope

Scope may be summarised as a statement of the context and extent of the HAZOP. In defining the scope, the study initiator should typically consider the following:

- The stage of the system's life cycle at which the study is to be carried out. This determines whether the study is preliminary or detailed; also whether results from previous studies will be relevant or necessary to it.

- The context of the study within the overall safety and hazard analyses of the system or of the plant of which the system is a component. This helps to identify previous relevant studies and to define the need to plan subsequent studies.
- Whether the study is to be complementary to previous studies, in which case their results should be available during the study, or contrasting with them, in which case it should be carried out independently of them. A contrasting study may be required if the results of one or more previous studies were suspect and an independent cross-check is needed.
- The extent of the threats to safety which the system could pose. In some cases, it may be justifiable for the study to be limited to the investigation of only a subset of the possible hazards, perhaps because of their degree of severity.
- The boundary of the system being studied. The term 'system' may be used to imply the entire plant or only a part of the plant. For example, a control system does not include the plant being controlled (though a HAZOP may need to consider the control system's effects on the controlled plant).
- The boundary of the study. The study may not extend to the boundary of the system under study, so it needs to be clearly defined.
- The number of design representations to be studied. There may be a number of representations of the design, each prepared for a given purpose, but the study may for some reason be limited to a subset of them. This would need to be clearly defined in the scope of the study.
- The nature of the design representations to be studied. Each type of representation provides information on certain, but not necessarily all, aspects of a system. For example, piping and instrumentation diagrams and data flow diagrams provide information on the flows but not on timing. If only such forms of representation are used, the scope of the study is limited to the aspects of a system included on them. Similarly, the level of detail offered by a design representation is a constraint on the scope of a study. Some representations, for example block diagrams, offer limited detail — but if this is considered sufficient in a given circumstance, a rapid and cost-effective study for a defined limited purpose may be possible and desirable.
- The required safety integrity level [IEC 98] of the system under study. Normally the SIL cannot be determined until some hazard

identification and analysis have been conducted, but once it has been determined, knowing it may be useful in defining which types of hazards are of particular interest.

- Legislation which is relevant to the system under development, the liability of the supplier, or the licensing of the operation of the system or the controlled plant.
- Any other systems with which the system is to be integrated or connected. The hazards relevant to the study may include those likely to be thrown up not only by the system being studied but also by those other systems.
- The purpose to which the results of the study will be put. The results of a HAZOP are typically used for informing system design. But they may also be used for determining the questions to ask a supplier, say of off-the-shelf software, or for improving the safety of an existing operational system.

A given statement of scope does not necessarily need to include all these issues. Nor should it be limited to these issues, which are merely examples of what might typically be considered in determining the scope of a HAZOP. It is the responsibility of the study initiator, having taken all relevant issues into consideration, to define the scope of the study. The study leader should then work within that scope.

5.4.2   Objectives

The objectives should define the purpose of the HAZOP and what the results of the study should provide. Typically, they should take the form of verb infinitives, e.g., 'An objective of the study is *to* ...'. Statements of objectives are intended to focus the study on those objectives to the exclusion of others, and thus to make the study effective. Being a team activity, a HAZOP is labour-intensive, so if unnecessary tasks can be avoided, the effectiveness of the study will be improved. Indeed, a study which is focused on a defined purpose is almost certainly carried out more quickly and cheaply than a 'general' study, so the definition of objectives is crucial to achieving cost-effectiveness.

The following issues should be considered when defining the objectives of a HAZOP, but it is not suggested that they are exhaustive.

- Whether the study is an overview study to provide initial information or a detailed study to provide definitive information on hazards. At a very early stage, the study may be for preliminary hazard identification; later in the development project, a detailed study may be required. A study limited to investigating the possible effects of changes to an operational system may be appropriate prior to making the changes.

- The types of hazard which the study is intended to identify. It is sometimes the case that a particular study is concerned not with all possible hazards but only with certain types, for example hazards to the environment, or to the public regardless of the hazards to the plant's staff or immediate environment.
- Whether it is required in this study to check if recommendations made in previous studies have been implemented or if measures have been taken to eliminate or mitigate previously identified hazards. If the study is complementary to a previous study, the results of the previous study should be available and a check on previous recommendations will be a normal part of the study.
- The context of this study within the overall hazard and safety analyses of the system or the total plant. The context aids the decision of what output will be needed from this study to inform future HAZOPs or other studies.

5.5   INITIAL PLANNING

Once the study leader has been briefed, he or she must carry out the initial planning of the study, supported by the study initiator. This includes selecting the study team, estimating the number of study meetings necessary, and proposing a schedule for them. The primary responsibility for ensuring that the planning is carried out should remain with the study initiator, who would normally delegate the actual planning to the study leader.

In selecting the study team (see Chapter 6 for details of this process), the availability of all members for the entire study must be established, for a study normally extends over a number of meetings. This implies securing the commitment of the managers of proposed team members. If the managers are to comply with the requests for their staff to be released from their regular duties, they require information well in advance, so at the time of the initial request they should be provided with the proposed meeting schedule. This reinforces the importance of carrying out adequate planning during the initiation stage of the study.

At the time that a HAZOP is initially identified as being necessary (perhaps at the commencement of a project), the study leader's identity may not be known, and there is no guarantee that he or she will possess the necessary authority to negotiate effectively with managers for the release of their staff. It is therefore imperative that study initiators are always of sufficient seniority and authority to do this. As there are other instances in which the support of the study initiator may be necessary, the study leader needs to be convinced at the initial briefing that he or she will receive that support.

A difficult task in the planning of a HAZOP is the estimation of the number of study meetings required, and this is considered in Chapter 8. Once an estimate has been made, a schedule of the meetings needs to be drawn up for the benefit of all those associated with the study. Typically, when this has been done, the study initiator may leave the more detailed planning to the study leader.

5.6   FOLLOW-UP WORK

Follow-up work may consist of resolving questions and acquiring information necessary to the continuation of the HAZOP, but it may also include the introduction of countermeasures against identified hazards and fulfilling other recommendations. Officially, a HAZOP ends at recommendations, so the former type of follow-up work is a necessary part of a study and the latter is not.

When it comes to follow-up work, the study leader may not have the authority to insist on the work being done and may, therefore, depend on the study initiator's support to ensure that effort is made available to carry out essential follow-up work (see Chapter 10). Indeed, effective continuation of the study may depend on this. The study initiator should therefore have the authority to facilitate essential follow-up work, and be prepared to use that authority. He or she may also have a role in monitoring any follow-up work which is not essential to the continuation of the current HAZOP but which is crucial to the safety of the system.

5.7   CLOSING THE STUDY

At the end of a HAZOP, the study initiator is responsible for checking that all study documentation has been compiled in accordance with the defined recording method and that it has been signed off by the study leader. Once this has been done, the study initiator should sign off the study in the manner appropriate to the organisation.

5.8   CONCLUDING REMARKS

The technical aspects of a HAZOP can in many circumstances be conducted quite smoothly without the intervention of a study initiator — just as it is quite possible to do a good job of any type without the formal intervention of quality assurance personnel. However, a study initiator with appropriate authority is invaluable to ensuring that HAZOPs are properly initiated, that they are successful, and that follow-up work is carried out — that is, that they are efficiently conducted, that they are carried out at the planned time or at the planned point in a project, and that they contribute effectively to the safety analysis of the system in question. Such a contribution by the study initiator can be crucial, for HAZOPs are expensive, and time and effort must not be squandered. In addition, identifying a study initiator in advance, and defining his or her responsibilities, builds checks into the HAZOP process — checks which can have huge implications for safety and its economical achievement.

To summarise, the main responsibilities of the study initiator are to:

• Ensure that the HAZOP is planned and carried out;
• Ensure that the timing of HAZOPs are defined in the project or operational plans;
• In the case of a development project, communicate with the project manager and follow the progress of the project, and in the case of an operational system, maintain awareness of the use and history of the system;
• Select and brief an appropriate study leader for each study;
• Make sure that the study leader becomes familiar with the purpose of the system and its representation and then, in the case of a development project, of its overall design, and in the case of an operational system, of its operational principles;
• Define the scope and objectives of the HAZOP;
• Carry out initial planning together with the study leader;
• Help the study leader to choose the members of the study team;
• Employ appropriate authority to ensure that the chosen team members are made available to participate in the study;
• Support the study leader in any way necessary to ensuring a successful study;

- Use authority to ensure that follow-up work is done;
- Check at the end of the study that the study documentation is complete and that it has been signed off by the study leader;
- Sign off the study.

6

Team Selection
and the Roles
of Team Members

This chapter describes the roles which must be filled by HAZOP team members, the activities which the team must perform, and the team selection process itself.

6.1 INTRODUCTION

A HAZOP is carried out by a team and is successful only if the team is well composed and well led. An experienced study leader, able to maintain control through firm chairmanship without sacrificing the harmony on which good teamwork depends, is essential.

The team itself is not homogeneous but requires its members to bring various skills pertinent both to carrying out a HAZOP in general and to studying a particular system. First, there are a number of core roles which must be filled if the team is to be complete. Then there are a number of activities which the team members between them must perform if the HAZOP is to be successful (see Chapter 9). The choice of appropriate team members is therefore crucial, not only for their individual skills but also for their complementarity.

It is not unusual for a HAZOP to be unsuccessful because of a lack of care in selecting the study leader or the team. Nor is it uncommon for an inefficient study to result from the acceptance of inappropriate team members because the first choices are 'too busy'. Although the human factors component of HAZOP has often been ignored or trivialised, it is in fact a crucial aspect of the process; if the team dynamics are not 'right', the study is likely to be both inefficient in detecting hazards and less cost-effective.

6.2   ROLES NECESSARY TO A HAZOP

In a HAZOP, each team member is chosen for one or more defined roles. Typically, the roles may be classified as:

- Study leader;
- Designer;
- User or intended user;
- Expert;
- Recorder.

As discussed in Chapter 5, the study leader is selected by the study initiator to be responsible for the planning and control of the study. His or her planning function and activities in controlling study meetings are described in Chapters 8 and 9 respectively. In the present context, the leader is responsible for selecting the team members, although, as mentioned in Chapter 5, he or she may require the support of the study initiator in obtaining their release from normal duties.

The designer, normally from the system design team, must have a good understanding of the design of the system under study and, importantly, of the design representation (or representations) being studied. At the start of the study, the designer is expected to remind the other team members of the principles of both. During the study, he or she has the task of explaining the intent of the design.

The user should be someone able to provide information on, and answer questions about, the operation of the system and the environment in which the system operates or will operate. For a system which is already operational, it is preferable for the user to be someone with direct operational and maintenance experience. For a system under development, the user could be a future operator of the system. However, intended operators are often not trained until the system is about to be brought into service and may therefore be unable fully to perform the role of user in studies carried out during development. In determining an appropriate user, the study leader needs to consider the scope and objectives of the study, because someone who would be a competent user in some circumstances or at one stage of the system's life cycle (say, when the system is in its conceptual stage) may not be competent in others (say, at an advanced stage of the design, when greater operational detail must be known).

'Experts' are team members selected for their specialist knowledge. They may be chosen for one or more of a number of reasons, among them:

- Their expertise in the exploration of deviations from design intent;
- Their understanding of the hazards which may be associated with the system;
- Their knowledge of systems similar to the one to be studied;
- Their knowledge of the system's environment;
- Their knowledge of the system or a part of the system;

The main purpose of expert members is to help the team to explore the possible causes and consequences of deviations during the study. If their expertise is in a part of the system only, they may need to be present only for a part of the HAZOP.

The recorder is the team member who documents what transpires at study meetings. To do this, he or she must understand the HAZOP process and be conversant with the type of system being studied and the design representation being used and its symbolism. As most HAZOPs are recorded on-line in a computer (see Section 9.7 of Chapter 9), the recorder needs to be a competent computer user and must also be totally fluent in the language (English, French, Korean, or whatever) in which the study is being conducted and documented.

If the recorder is inadequate in any respect, the documentation of the proceedings will be slow and subject to error and the efficiency of the study compromised. The recorder needs to work closely with the study leader, as a secretary at any meeting must do with the chairman. On occasions the study leader may delegate to the recorder the responsibility of acquiring the documentation from previous studies and making it available at the current study, in which case the recorder would need to become familiar with it so as to explain its results to the team members. Throughout a HAZOP, the recorder must document the conclusions, recommendations and questions which emerge from the study process. Although the recorder will have the benefit of the study leader's summaries and conclusions of what has taken place, he or she needs to be competent at summarising and recording, in concise prose, the key points of what could be a complex discussion. Possible recording styles which may be used are discussed in Chapter 10.

The study leader and the recorder normally need to be dedicated to their roles, but, otherwise, there is no reason in principle why team members should not combine two or more roles.

6.3   ACTIVITIES IMPLICIT IN THE PROCESS

Each time a guide word is applied in a HAZOP, a process is enacted. This consists of five activities:

- Postulation of a possible deviation from design intent;
- Exploration of the deviation's possible causes and consequences;
- Explanation of issues relevant to the postulated deviation from design intent, such as the behaviour of the system, problems known with similar systems, and any relevant protection or alarm mechanisms in place or planned;
- Summarising results and drawing conclusions about whether a hazard exists;
- Recording the results.

Each stage of this process requires a particular skill, and each skill is necessary to the success of the study and should be possessed by at least one of the team members. The leader is normally responsible for postulating deviations and drawing conclusions, and the recorder for documenting the results. There are no firm rules as to who should possess each of the other skills. However, in a typical HAZOP, they might be expected to be distributed as follows (and see Figure 6.1).

- The study leader would postulate the possible deviation and, in some cases, might be competent to explore deviations and explain their significance;
- The expert members would be competent explorers of the causes and effects of deviations within the system, and also able to explain these phenomena;

	Postulate	Explore	Explain	Conclude	Record
Leader	Yes	Possibly	Possibly	Yes	
Expert		Yes	Yes		
Designer		Possibly	Yes		
User		Possibly	Yes		
Recorder		Possibly			Yes

Figure 6.1: Key activities and their likely possessors

- The designer too might be a competent explorer, but should certainly be capable of explaining the design intent, how defined problems could be caused, and how the system would behave in their presence;
- The user might also be an explorer, but would be expected to explain what the operational interactions and consequences of a defined deviation could be, not only with respect to the system but also to its environment, and the extent to which they may be hazardous;
- The study leader would summarise the results and draw conclusions;
- The recorder would document the results of the exploration;
- The study leader would keep track of concerns which need to be studied on another design representation or in a future study (see Chapter 12).

6.4   THE STUDY LEADER

6.4.1   Credentials of a Study Leader

A HAZOP is superficially simple, but its success depends on careful planning and team selection, sensitive but firm control of study meetings, and meticulous attention to detail in the investigation of deviations from design intent. An appropriate combination of qualities in the study leader is therefore necessary. Persons with lesser credentials are often able to lead HAZOPs with apparent success, but almost always problems occur and time is wasted — and almost always it is not recognised that these troubles could have been overcome by a more appropriate choice of leader, with the result that the HAZOP process itself is blamed. This leads to a self-perpetuating spiral of poor management of HAZOP, followed by distrust in the process, and an unwillingness to invest adequately in it. This in turn can lead to unsatisfactory studies with poor results, and the 'justified' abandonment of the technique.

The principal attributes necessary in a study leader include:

- A good understanding of the HAZOP process. This requires a theoretical knowledge, the experience of participation in many previous studies, and appropriate training (see Section 6.4.2).

- Experience in leading HAZOPs. Of course there must be a first time for every leader, but this should be supervised (again see Section 6.4.2).

- Competence in planning. A HAZOP can extend over a number of meetings, and the preparation for the study (see Chapter 8) and the planning of the meeting schedule can be complex.

- Competence as a chairperson. The purpose of a HAZOP is to identify hazards, and the study team is gathered for that purpose. Time should therefore not be diverted to other purposes, such as designing countermeasures against identified hazards. If it is, inevitably only a minority of team members will be involved and the majority will be excluded. This wastes time, leads to frustration, and diminishes concentration and team spirit, both of which are essential ingredients of a successful study. Firm control of meetings is therefore necessary. The desire to discuss extraneous matters is always present, and the study leader must be conscious of the need to return the discussion to the main purpose of the study without antagonising the team members, for doing so would also lead to a loss of concentration and team spirit.

- Sensitivity to human feelings. It is not unusual for the identification of hazards to be perceived as a form of criticism of the system design. It is then not unnatural for the designer to respond defensively. The study leader needs to ensure that questioning of the design is not presented, or interpreted, as criticism of the designer. While being sensitive to the designer's feelings, he or she must also limit any defensive response so that time is not wasted. Defence of the design is not a good use of time at a HAZOP.

- Independence of the system being studied. This is a preferred attribute rather than a mandatory one, but it is often the case that the study leader is able to take a more system-wide view and to control the study meetings more closely if he or she is not deeply involved in the development project or the operational system. However, the study leader should be sufficiently familiar with the system's technical field and its design representations to direct and control the study without faltering.

- Attention to detail. Hazards are to be found in the details of the design representation as well as on its surface. The maximum number of hazards can be identified only by a meticulous study. If the study leader is impatient of detail and superficial in outlook, he or she is unlikely to lead a thorough study.

6.4.2   Training for the Study Leader

With a number of meetings in the study schedule and several team members present at each, a HAZOP is not cost-free. If its cost is to be minimised, the attributes listed in the section above need to be present in the study leader. If they are not, training is necessary in the following disciplines:

- Planning — indeed, training and experience in project management is an advantage to a study leader;
- Chairmanship of meetings;
- HAZOP — this training should be based not only on a theoretical understanding of HAZOP but also, and importantly, on practical experience.

Given that a potential leader possesses the necessary credentials, the following is considered to comprise the minimum basic training:

- First, performing the role of recorder for at least 30 hours over at least 15 HAZOP study sessions;
- Then, performing the role of leader, in collaboration with and supported by a recorder who is a trained leader, for at least 12 hours over at least 6 HAZOP study sessions;
- Finally, being monitored by and having to report to a trained and experienced study leader for at least the next 20 study hours, over at least ten HAZOP study sessions.

Adequate training may be difficult to arrange quickly if a person who seems otherwise to be an appropriate study leader requires it, so it is best for an organisation to be prepared in advance by maintaining a pool of accredited study leaders. Then, only familiarisation with the system to be studied and its design representations would be needed as preparation for a particular study.

6.5   TEAM SELECTION

Given the briefing by the study initiator, and the scope and objectives which have been determined for the study, the study leader has the responsibility for selecting the most appropriate study team. In doing so, he or she needs to:

- Find people with the knowledge or experience of the system under study and the ability to perform the roles essential to HAZOP (see Section 6.2);
- Ensure that the potential team members are between them capable of performing the activities implicit in a HAZOP (see Section 6.3);
- Ensure that the team is balanced so that it makes for a cost-effective study (see Section 6.5.3).

6.5.1 Filling the Roles

In determining the requirements of a HAZOP, it is beneficial for the study leader to review, with the designer (and the study initiator if necessary), the system design and the particular design representations to be used in the study. Then, the skills necessary in the team members can be deduced and the study leader can define the criteria for choosing appropriate persons to fill the roles.

The roles of designer and user should always be filled. In some cases the designer or user may play an expert role as well, but other experts should be omitted from the team only if it is certain that they would not add anything to the process. In considering the role of the designer, it is useful to note that the same person would not necessarily be appropriate at all stages of the system life cycle, or even at all meetings of a given study. This is particularly true when the study is to cover the whole or a large part of an extensive system. Design is usually carried out by a team, and the details of some sub-systems may be understood only by those who have worked on them.

In selecting a user, someone with operational experience and understanding, and a knowledge of the system's operational environment or intended environment, should be sought. If the system has already been in operation, an operator would often be most appropriate. In aviation, for example, a pilot would be the operator. When the system is still in development, it may be the case that operators have not yet been appointed, or trained, so someone planning the training courses for operators, or someone preparing the environment in which the operators will work, may be suitable. Or someone who has operated a similar system (for example an older version of the system) in a similar environment might be appropriate. So a train driver who has operated a manually controlled train might be a suitable user in a study of an automatic train control system.

When it comes to the selection of experts, judgement on the part of the team leader is called for. Often it may seem that the designer and user between them already possess all the knowledge that is required. But other areas of expertise which may be useful or necessary may be provided by: the supplier of the system, the developer of the system or its software, or the maintainer of the system. Moreover, an expert may be selected because of a knowledge of safety engineering, or investigative techniques, as much as because of a knowledge of the system under study. The study leader needs to identify the possible gaps in the team's abilities, and plan how they can be filled by the inclusion of appropriate experts.

The recorder clearly needs to be good at following a detailed technical discussion, getting to the core of it, and quickly summarising its results in good prose. Further, if the recorder is to use modern technology in recording and reproducing the results of the HAZOP, he or she needs to be adept in its operation.

During the course of a study (from meeting to meeting), the team may grow and shrink, as users, designers and experts are called in for the analysis of different parts of the design. But there should be a balance between:

- Allowing change in order to introduce the right expertise;
- Achieving consistency across study meetings or studies by maintaining a core team;
- Keeping the size of the team to a cost-effective and manageable level (see Section 6.5.3).

Having chosen the appropriate team members, the study leader should invite them by name and obtain their agreement, and that of their managers, that they will participate for the entire schedule of study meetings — or for those meetings for which their participation is required.

It goes without saying that all team members should be familiar with the types of design representation to be used in the study, and if this is not the case a design familiarisation exercise may need to be carried out. Familiarity with the HAZOP process is also a necessity, but while the study will progress faster if this has been gained in advance, it is possible for members to acquire it at the initial stage of the study.

6.5.2   Ensuring the Activities

In selecting team members, the study leader needs to ensure not only their active participation but also that between them they are able to contribute the necessary abilities: to postulate a deviation from design intent, to explore its possible causes and consequences, to explain relevant issues, to draw conclusions from the exploration and explanation, and to summarise and record the main issues.

Whether a team member can perform one of the essential activities in a given context depends on his or her previous knowledge and experience as well as on his personality. Each team member should have a perception of filling one of the roles of designer, expert, user, or recorder. It is the study leader's responsibility to ensure, in selecting the team, that the ability to perform each of the activities is present and, in conducting the study, that it is deployed appropriately. Except in the case of the recorder, the study leader should not formally designate the responsibility for carrying out an activity to a particular team member, but rather, while selecting the team, ensure that the abilities and propensities to carry them out are possessed by the team members. Having said that, it should be added that the chosen experts should be competent explorers; that is their function. There is no point in having experts who are not logical and creative, who cannot express themselves clearly, or who do not come to the point, however much they know. Similarly, a designer who cannot explain the intent of each characteristic of the design, or a user who cannot explain operational and environmental issues, is unlikely to be of benefit to the study. The study leader should not only chose team members with these issues in mind but should also brief them accordingly prior to the study.

6.5.3   Team Balance and Cost-effectiveness

As well as the technical competence of the team members, there are a number of other issues which the study leader must consider in selecting the team.

(a)   The Right People

A frequent problem at a HAZOP is that the selected (and agreed) team members do not turn up for one or more meetings, but send a replacement instead. This can have one or more detrimental effects:

- It causes delay to the meeting because the new member is not familiar with the system under study, or its representation, or with the HAZOP process;
- It causes delay because the new member needs to be 'brought up to speed' and requires a repeat of what has already been done;

- It reduces the effectiveness of the study because the new member almost always does not possess the knowledge for which the choice of the original member was made;
- It reduces the efficiency of the process because the team has been disrupted. This effect is often overlooked, but it is of considerable importance. A team develops its own dynamics, and it has a life cycle over which its dynamics evolve. It takes time to develop into a smooth-running, harmonious and productive unit. When its composition is changed, particularly for a reason which is perceived to be inadequate, it reverts from a mode of 'productivity' to one of 'formation'. A great deal of time can be wasted by this reversion, and hazards may be missed because of it.

In seeking the release of the appropriate team members for the duration of the study, the study leader needs to provide the study schedule to the intended members and their managers. This in turn implies that the study should already have been planned (see Chapter 8). If there is any doubt as to the adequacy of the study leader's authority in securing the prospective members' release, the support of the study initiator should be sought. Of course, there are times when it is not possible to secure the most appropriate person, but this should be established at the outset so that a second choice can be recruited for the full study schedule. Once team membership has been agreed, it should be honoured.

It is important that managers agree to release appropriate staff for the HAZOP if at all possible and that they then adhere to their promises to do so. On this issue, two points are worth making. First, if an organisation is serious about achieving safety, and if a real safety culture exists within the organisation, it will be recognised that the success of a HAZOP demands suitable team members and not merely team members who happen to be available at the time. Second, once a manager has agreed to release staff to carry out a study, retraction of the promise can cause not only a less effective study but also the waste of a great deal of other people's time.

Substitutes should not be accepted at the last minute, unless it is certain that their contributions to the study would be, if not as effective as those of the original appointees, at least adequately effective. Achieving this state of affairs is not an easy matter in organisations in which there is not a safety culture or a culture of keeping one's word. If safety is a product attribute which is not accorded a high priority, or if the late breach of a promise is considered acceptable, there will always be a high likelihood of managers not honouring their agreements to release staff for HAZOP. But if HAZOP is to be effective both in identifying hazards and in cost terms, a culture of safety and integrity needs to exist.

At the same time, it should also be recognised that from time to time a team member may be forced to miss a meeting or to withdraw from the study for some valid reason. The study leader should therefore appoint a number of reserve team members for various roles, particularly those of expert, in case there is a last-minute need for them. A study can be seriously disrupted, and rendered both inefficient and ineffective, if inappropriate replacement members are allowed to participate.

(b) Optimum Team Size

We have found the optimum team size to be between four and seven, including the study leader, depending on the circumstances. Fewer than four members is almost certain to represent insufficient viewpoints to guarantee a complete study. More than seven almost always involves too much overlap of viewpoints, resulting in either too repetitive an exploration of hazards or too many members not contributing to the proceedings. For the team to function effectively, all members must be involved in the exploration. When one or more is 'left out' for too long, they are likely to lose interest and concentration and to 'switch off'. The study then loses the advantage of their presence. A HAZOP can be difficult enough to control with a team of optimum size; the study leader adds difficulty (as well as cost) by including or allowing too many members in the team.

It should be admitted, however, that there may be special cases when it is deemed appropriate to field a much larger team. One study of which we are aware was of the interfaces between three major systems, each of which had already been subjected to a detailed HAZOP. The team for the interface HAZOP was 20 strong, and the study occupied two sessions per day for three days, at the end of which the experienced team leader was exhausted.

(c) Choice of Experts

The team leader needs to reflect carefully on the choice of expert team members. First there is the simple matter of cost. Each team member adds to the cost of the study, and too much redundancy means that the study is costing more than it should, as explained in (b) above.

There is no reason why a team member should not perform two functions. In some cases the study leader may play the role of an expert.

Or a designer or user might also be selected to be an expert, on some occasions because he is the most appropriate person anyway, and on others because the advantage of including another expert is outweighed by that of reducing the size of the team. At the same time, it is an advantage to have at lease one explorer other than the designer, particularly when the second explorer is a specialist in a field essential to the study.

(d)   Team Consistency

There are three aspects of team consistency. The first is across the several meetings of a study. The second concerns the use of more than one design representation in a study and therefore the need for different viewpoints or spheres of knowledge — which might require different team members. The third is across the HAZOPs at the different stages of the life cycle of the same system.

The importance of maintaining consistency throughout the meetings of a HAZOP has already been emphasised. A team takes time to become efficiently productive, and changes can retard progress or reverse development. Thus, prior to the study meetings, the study leader needs to plan the continued involvement of members. Then, during the meetings he or she needs to motivate the team both to evolve quickly and to function efficiently. Nevertheless, there are times when new team members are needed for particular purposes or a resigning member needs to be replaced. Then the study leader should select a replacement who will rapidly be integrated into the team without disrupting its harmony or interrupting its efficiency, and who will contribute effectively to the process without threatening the contributions of the other members.

Occasionally, too, a new member needs to be brought in for one or a few meetings, as a designer, user or expert, to answer particular questions or provide assistance with respect to given parts of the system, such as third-party software. In such cases it is sometimes better for the harmony of the existing team if the study leader does not attempt to integrate the newcomer into the team but allows them to be perceived as a helpful stranger. Then the advantage of the newcomer's presence is gained while the disadvantage of introducing him or her as a 'new member' is avoided.

Whether or not there is consistency of membership across the meetings, and whether or not helpful strangers are brought in for some meetings, the leadership of the study leader is the glue which binds the team together. Team spirit and motivation must be maintained, and it is the study leader who must inculcate them into the HAZOP process.

The use of more than one design representation of the system in a study introduces a further problem in maintaining consistency. If greatly different skills are not required for the study of the different representations, the study leader may decide to study them at the same meeting, with the advantage that a given entity may be examined on all the representations simultaneously. Doing this increases the chance of achieving consistency in the team from meeting to meeting. When different skills are required, less time is wasted if separate meetings are arranged for the study of the different design representations. However, consistency is still required across their study, and a core team should be defined. Then, as the team changes across meetings, or grows or shrinks as experts are called in to deal with particular matters and are then excused, this core maintains both team spirit and continuity in the study.

How these matters are handled must depend on the circumstances and on the skill and personality of the study leader. It is emphasised, however, that the study leader needs to be alert to the delicacy of team dynamics and the importance of their being 'right'.

It is somewhat more difficult to achieve consistency across studies at the different stages of the life cycle of the same system, for these may be separated in time, perhaps by years. However, it is an advantage if some consistency can be achieved. The study initiator should keep this in mind in choosing a study leader, and the study leader in selecting a team. Further, the documentation of each HAZOP should be stored so that it is available and understandable to future studies.

6.6 CONCLUDING REMARKS

The human element is crucial to a HAZOP, and team dynamics, although often ignored in favour of 'getting the job done', are key to its success. In setting up the study, the study initiator needs to select the team leader not because of his or her position in the organisation but because of an ability to plan and control the study and to lead the study team harmoniously and effectively.

In planning the study, the study leader needs to select team members not only because of their expertise but also with a view to their contributing to a team effort, and to discharging the activities implicit in HAZOP.

This chapter has identified the necessary roles of HAZOP team members, the activities which must be carried out for a successful study, and the factors affecting the selection of a study team.

7
The Use of Guide Words

This chapter describes the use of guide words to investigate the possible deviations of attributes from their design intent. This is a key part of the rigorous and systematic procedure that is a HAZOP. A guide word is a word or phrase which expresses and defines a specific type of deviation from design intent. The guide word is used as a prompt, to focus the study and elicit ideas and discussion, and thus to maximise the chance of identifying and studying all possible hazards.

In this chapter, a set of guide words, which has been found to be comprehensive, is described. An explanation of the importance of interpreting the guide words in context is followed by a section on how the guide words should facilitate the process and not constrain it. The remainder of the chapter (Section 7.4 onwards) discusses the choice of attribute-guide-word interpretations when the system under scrutiny contains programmable electronics (i.e. systems containing software) and gives some examples of their use.

7.1 A SET OF GUIDE WORDS

Experience over many years has shown that the use of guide words helps both to direct and to stimulate the creative process of exploring potential deviations. There is a set of guide words which is generic in the process industries [CIA 77] which is:

- No: this is the complete negation of the design intention — no part of the intention is achieved, but nothing else happens;
- More: this is a quantitative increase;
- Less: this is a quantitative decrease;
- As well as: this is a qualitative increase, where all the design intention is achieved together with additional activity;
- Part of: this is a qualitative decrease, where only part of the design intention is achieved;
- Reverse: this is the logical opposite of the intention;
- Other than: this is a complete substitution, where no part of the original intention is achieved but something quite different happens.

When it is relevant to examine timing as part of a HAZOP, additional guide words are needed. We recommend the following which become added to our generic set:

- Early: something happens earlier in time than intended;
- Late: something happens later in time than intended;
- Before: something happens earlier in a sequence than intended;
- After: something happens later in a sequence than intended.

As will be explained in Chapter 8, it is the responsibility of the study leader in preparing for the study to examine the design representations to be studied, identify the attributes which arise from them and select appropriate guide words from the above lists. The guide words chosen and their interpretations (see Section 7.2) must match the system being examined and the design representations. Some of the generic guide words given above may not be appropriate for particular attributes in particular applications. For example, the guide words 'as well as' and 'part of' are not applicable to the attribute 'speed' of an electric motor; for the attribute 'data flow' on a data flow diagram, the guide word 'less' is not used as its meaning is covered by 'part of'. The study leader should therefore produce the list of guide words and interpretations and distribute them to the members of the study team in advance of the study.

7.2   THE GUIDE WORDS MUST BE INTERPRETED IN CONTEXT

In our early work on applying HAZOP in areas other than the process industries, first to electromechanical systems and then to electronics-based designs and programmable systems, we found that we were inventing new guide words in order to cope with the rich set of deviations possible in the different systems. Those HAZOPs were successful, but we gradually came to realise that what we were actually doing each time was not generating a new guide word but putting a particular interpretation on one of the generic guide words; each interpretation being dependent on the context of the system and the attributes of the design representation under study. The conclusion is that the generic set of guide words is normally usable — given that the guide words are interpreted in the particular defined context.

Guide words may be interpreted differently in different industries, at different stages of the system's life cycle, and when applied to different design representations. This is a key point. The interpretation of a guide word needs to be in the context of these factors.

It is the responsibility of the study leader, usually working with one of the designers or someone who knows the design representation well, to examine the design representation in the context of the other factors (such as the industry and the stage of the life cycle) and define the interpretations of each of the guide words for each attribute of the entities on the representation. Some guide words may have no meaningful interpretation in the given context and some may have more than one valid interpretation. Here are two examples. Firstly, for the attribute 'data flow' in a computer system, possible interpretations of 'more' are: 'data may be passed at a higher rate than intended' and 'more data is passed than intended'. In fact, here the attribute of 'data flow' could be more accurately expressed as two attributes, one of 'data rate' and the other of 'data quantity'.

Secondly, for the attribute of 'wire capability' in an electronic circuit, the guide word 'more' can mean 'too high voltage' or 'too high current'.

It is important that the interpretations are chosen during preparation before the HAZOP meeting at which they are to be used and circulated to the team members in advance so as to avoid protracted discussion at the study meetings.

An effective way to derive appropriate interpretations is to take the generic meaning of each guide word given in Section 7.1 and to think what interpretation of the guide word best expresses its meaning in the given context (with respect to the attribute in question and the nature of the system). A few examples of the interpretations of specific guide words for different attributes may illustrate this:

- No: the generic meaning is that no part of the intention is achieved.
  - For the attribute of 'flow' of a substance in a pipe between two vessels in a chemical plant, this will mean that no flow takes place.
  - For an electrical signal between two components and the attribute of 'voltage' across them, the deviation might be interpreted as the total absence of a signal, or zero volts.
  - For the interconnection between two processes on a data flow diagram and the attributes of either a 'data flow' or a 'control flow', the deviation might be that no data or control signal is passed.
- Part of: the generic meaning is a qualitative decrease where only part of the design intention is achieved.
  - For flow of two or more substances in a pipe on a chemical plant, this could be interpreted as one or more substances being missing from the mixture.
  - For voltage, the guide word 'part of' is usually not applicable, but when the entity under consideration is an amplitude-modulated signal, the interpretation of 'part of' might be that the voltage is present but there is no modulation.
  - For data flow or control flow on a data flow diagram, an interpretation is that the data or control signal is incomplete.
  - For frequency shift keying signals, the interpretation would be that no shift is applied but the frequency is present.

The interpretations for a specific study may be presented in a number of ways. For instance, many people use a list. In our work we have found that an effective way to present the interpretations is as a matrix, with the guide words as column headings, the attributes being examined as the row titles, and the interpretations filling the cells. Examples of these are given later in this chapter.

It is important that the set of attributes, guide words and interpretations is:

- Understood by all members of the team, otherwise each team member will not be able to play a full role in the HAZOP;
- Applied consistently, to provide assurance that the HAZOP is being carried out rigorously;
- Sufficient to explore plausible deviations from design intent — this

is such an important point that it is expanded on in Section 7.3 below, which also covers the introduction of new guide words or interpretations during a study.

7.3   INTERPRETATIONS ARE TO FACILITATE NOT CONSTRAIN

The purpose of the interpretations of the guide words is to enable the exploration of plausible deviations from design intent. The examples given in this chapter and in Chapters 13 and 15 are derived from successful HAZOPs which we have carried out. However, other interpretations are not precluded (see, for example, the work carried out at the University of Teesside [Fencott 94] and the University of York [McDermid 94, 95]).

Some practitioners, particularly in the field of PES, have engaged in much debate on which is the theoretically correct set of guide words and interpretations for each design representation. This, we believe, comes from a misplaced focus on the guide words themselves rather than on the use of the attribute-guide-word interpretation combinations. It is not more and more guide words that are required, but interpretations of a limited set of guide words that are appropriate to the situation in hand. The aim of the HAZOP is to identify hazards and the attribute-guide-word interpretations are facilitators of the process.

The guide words are intended to prompt the creative exploration by team members of deviations from the design intent of components or the interconnections between components. The choice of interpretations must be adequate to allow this creative exploration. There is no universal 'right' set of interpretations. As a general guide, the interpretations need to be broad enough to allow imaginative exploration of deviations by the team. Our experience over many years of doing HAZOPs in a wide variety of industries and application areas is that interpretations which are too 'tight' tend to hinder this creative exploration.

The use of HAZOP in programmable systems is fairly new and best practice is still evolving. In this area in particular it would be wrong to be too prescriptive about interpretations: extensive experience by many practitioners over a number of years will be necessary to enable a consensus to be built up of best practice.

In the authors' experience, the use of a totally new guide word has never been necessary. However, on occasions, during a HAZOP meeting, it may become apparent that exploring a particular deviation from design intent throws up the need for one of the generic set of guide words that has not been included in the original study list to be used or for a new interpretation of one of the chosen guide words. The study leader must decide if the additional guide word or interpretation is a valid one to use for the attribute in question or whether it is a special case applicable only to the particular item being examined. If the former, the study leader should introduce the additional interpretation or guide word and ask the recorder to document the reasons for doing so. Of course, introducing an additional guide word or interpretation in the middle of a meeting or a series of meetings means that it has not been applied earlier, so it is recommended that the parts of the system examined to date be reviewed using the additional guide word or interpretation.

7.4   GUIDE WORDS AND THEIR INTERPRETATIONS FOR PES

The remainder of this chapter applies some of the above principles to a variety of representations that are common when considering systems that include a programmable electronic system (PES) — but the examples, by extension, are generally applicable. As well as the programmable parts, it is necessary to consider the electronic systems of which they are part and the electromechanical systems which they control or interface with. Thus the following are considered:

- Software using data flow diagrams;
- Software using state transition diagrams;
- Timing issues of repetition and response time;
- Software using object-oriented diagrams;
- Electronic hardware;
- Communication networks;
- Electromechanical systems.

7.4.1   Software Using Data Flow Diagrams

Data flow diagrams are used widely in many of the software design methodologies that come under the broad title of 'structured design'. We have found data flow diagrams particularly useful for generating design representations that are easily understandable by non-computer experts. In Figure 7.1 we show a common convention, using a subset of the Hatley-Pirbhai methodology [Hatley 88] which has been changed to show the entities of data flow and control flow on the same diagram.

On the diagram each process is shown in a circle with the number of

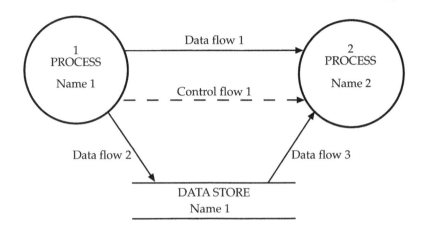

Figure 7.1: Data flow/control flow diagram

the process (here it is '1' or '2') and the process name (e.g. PROCESS Name 1). The data flows are shown by solid lines between the processes with an arrow showing the direction of flow. Control flow is shown by a dotted line. Data stores are shown as two parallel horizontal lines with the data store name between them.

A software design presented as data flow diagrams is usually hierarchical, with each process at a high level being decomposed into lower-level processes, with an associated greater level of detail for some of the data flows. Thus a HAZOP of lower levels of detail will look inside the processes defined at the higher level.

It is convenient to think of data flows as being intermittent or continuous. In the Hatley-Pirbhai methodology control flows are always intermittent. During a HAZOP it is useful to distinguish between data and control flows when examining credible deviations.

The attributes of the interconnections on a data flow or control flow diagram that are normally examined are: flow (of data or control), data rate and data value. Sample interpretations for these are shown in Table 7.1 later in this chapter.

Some practitioners have experienced difficulty with compound data flows or other interconnections between components on a PES design. This often arises on data flow diagrams where the flow on an interconnection may be anything from a single data item to a group of any number of items. On a high-level diagram, a single title may be descriptive of the whole group, with decomposition into subgroups and then into primitive single-item flows taking place on successively more detailed design representations. The handling of such compound flows during a HAZOP is postponed to Chapter 12 as it does not normally affect the choice of guide words or interpretations.

7.4.2 Software Using State Transition Diagrams

Finite state machines recognise that many processes may be in a number of states (an aircraft, say, could be in the states of 'stationary', 'taxi-ing', 'taking-off', 'in-flight' or 'landing', and a valve could be in the states of 'open', 'closed', 'opening', or 'closing'). Finite state machines (often using state transition diagrams) give the 'rules' for how transitions between states occur. In any given state, when an event occurs that is associated with a transition from that state, the machine will go to the state indicated by the transition and will perform the associated action. The Hatley-Pirbhai methodology uses a model for state transition diagrams in which the actions are associated with the transition.

Figure 7.2 shows a common convention for a state transition diagram. States are shown as rectangular boxes containing the state names. 'Transition arcs' are lines with arrowheads showing the directions of the transitions. 'Events' are the initiating conditions for transitions shown by name as labels on the arcs of the transitions they cause. 'Actions' are shown by name, adjacent to the events that cause them, with the two separated by a diagonal line (e.g. event/action). One state is the start state.

For a state transition diagram the relevant attributes to examine are

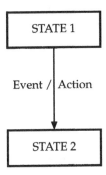

Figure 7.2: Convention for state transition diagrams

Table 7.1: Example guide word interpretations for data flow diagrams and state transition diagrams

	No	More	Less	As well as	Part of	Reverse	Other than	Early	Late	Before	After
Generic meanings	no part of the intention is achieved	a quantitative increase	a quantitative decrease	all design intent but with additional results	only some of the intention is achieved	the logical opposite of the intention	result other than original intention is achieved	relative to clock time	relative to clock time	related to order or sequence	related to order or sequence
For PES attributes of data flow and control flow	no data or control signal passed	more data is passed than expected			the information passed is incomplete (for group flows)	generally not credible	information complete but incorrect	flow of information occurs before it was intended	flow of information occurs after it was intended		
Attribute of data value for data flow diagram		value too high (within or out of bounds)	value is too low (within or out of bounds)								
Attribute of data rate for data flow diagram		the data rate is too high	the data rate is too low								
Attributes of events / actions and their timings for state transition diagrams	event does not happen or no action takes place			another event or an additional (unwanted) action takes place as well	an incomplete action is performed (not usually credible for events)		unexpected event instead of that anticipated or an incorrect action takes place	event / action takes place before it is expected	event / action takes place after it is expected	happens before another event or action that is expected to precede it	happens after another event or action that is expected to come after it
Attribute of response time (with timing diagram)	never happens (time infinite)	time longer than required	time shorter than required	synchronisation with other I/O gives problems			time is variable				

the events which initiate transitions between states and the actions that accompany those transitions. Often, some information on timing will also be available and then the additional attribute of the timing of the event or action can be examined. Sample interpretations of these attributes are given in Table 7.1, together with those for data flow diagrams.

7.4.3 Timing Issues of Repetition and Response Time

When real-time systems are being designed, there is often the need to define some characteristics of the timing. In the Hatley-Pirbhai methodology, two attributes of timing that are given are repetition time and response time. Repetition time is the time between successive updates of external primitive outputs. Response time is the time from input to output.

Examples of repetition time are the need to release the brakes every 50 msec on the ABS system of a car so as to avoid wheel-lock, and the requirement to update commands to the traction system of an automated train every 0.5 seconds. Using the same applications as examples of response time, we could have the time taken between the car driver putting a foot on the brake at a certain pressure and the brakes being applied, and the time taken between the train passing a trackside communications point to taking action based on that communication (say responding to a message to slow down to a given speed). Possible interpretations of the guide words for these attributes are given in Table 7.2.

Table 7.2: Example guide-word interpretations for the attributes of 'repetition time' and 'response time'

Attribute	Guide word	Interpretation
Repetition time	No	Output is not updated
	More	Time between outputs is longer than required
	Less	Time between outputs is shorter than required
	Other than	Time between outputs is variable
Response time	No	Never happens (time infinite)
	More	Time is longer than required
	Less	Time is shorter than required
	Other than	Time is variable

7.4.4   Software Using Object Oriented Analysis

The use of object oriented design methods has increased rapidly in recent years because it is a useful and appropriate way of modelling many types of systems. At the moment there are many different notations and approaches used and none has become dominant. The notation proposed by Shlaer and Mellor [Shlaer 92] has been used in a number of real-time analyses and designs for safety-related systems and is the basis of the following examples.

There are two main activities, analysis and design. Analysis is dealt with in the rest of this section and one of the examples in Chapter 15 uses object oriented design. A complete analysis using the Shlaer-Mellor approach comprises four basic models:

- An information model (commonly called an entity relationship diagram);
- State transition diagrams for each object with dynamic behaviour;
- An object communication model, to show the event communication between objects;
- An object access model, to show the synchronous communication between objects.

Note that in this section the word 'entity' has its specific object oriented meaning, not that used in the remainder of this book.

(a)   Entity Relationship Diagram

A simple example of the convention used for the entity relationship diagram is shown in Figure 7.3. An object is an abstraction of a set of real-world things where all the things in the set (the instances) have the same characteristics.

In Figure 7.3, object 1 is a lady and object 2 is a diamond ring. The

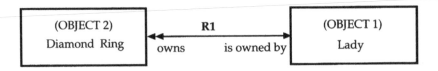

Figure 7.3: Relationship between a lady and a diamond ring

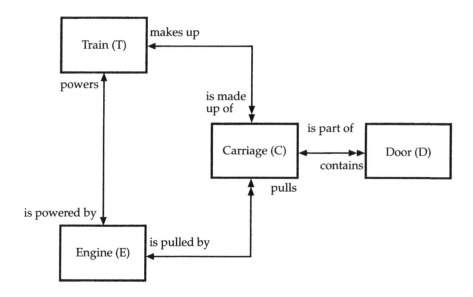

Figure 7.4: A more complex example showing some parts of a train

relationship between the two is shown by the arrowed line with the annotation on each end defining the relationship. Thus, a lady 'owns' one or more diamond rings (the double arrow signifies that there are potentially a number of instances of diamond ring associated with each lady) but each diamond ring is owned by one lady (hence the single arrow at that end). Of course, real examples will be rather more complex and Figure 7.4 shows the relationships between the entities of a train, the carriages on the train and the engine that pulls the train.

It can be seen from the examples above that when we are considering the possible deviations from design intent, those deviations may be in the objects themselves or in the relationships between the objects. Relationships may be conditional or unconditional. In a conditional relationship, there are instances of objects that do not participate. An unconditional relationship is one where every instance of an object is required to participate in the relationship. As an example, consider the relationships between a company, its employees and the spouses of the employees. The relationship between company and employee is 'employs' and clearly this is unconditional because every employee, by definition, is employed by the company. The relationship between employee and spouse is 'is married to' and this is conditional on the spouse side because there will be instances

Table 7.3: Example attribute-guide-word interpretation for entity relationships

Attribute	Guide word	Interpretation
Relationship	No	Relationship does not take place
	More/Less	Wrong cardinality in a relationship (for example it is one to one instead of one to many)
	Part of (i)	The set of relationships held by an entity shows incompatibilities between individual relations
	Part of (ii)	There is a required relationship that is not shown on the design
	Other than (i)	The wrong relationship is defined between objects (i.e. there should be a relationship between the objects, but not the one given)
	Other than (ii)	Relationship is wrong (i.e. there should not be a relationship between the objects even though one is given)

of employees who are not married, but there cannot be a spouse without an associated employee.

Unconditional relationships may be of the following forms of cardinality:

- One to one, where a single instance of an object is associated with a single instance of another (e.g. husband and wife);
- One to many, where a single instance of an object is associated with one or more instances of another, and each instance of the second is associated with just one instance of the first (e.g. the lady and diamond ring relationship of Figure 7.3);
- Many to many, where a single instance of an object is associated with one or more instances of another and each instance of the second object is associated with one or more instances of the first (e.g. houses and owners).

Possible guide word interpretations for the attribute of relationship are shown in Table 7.3. Here the guide words related to timing have no valid interpretation, and neither do 'as well as' and 'reverse'. The interpretation for 'no' is clear and the interpretations for 'more' and 'less' come from the different types of cardinality described above.

However, there are two different interpretations for the guide words 'part of' and 'other than'. The first one for 'part of' comes from a possible incompatibility between relationships (e.g. the entity 'child' may have a relationship shown to 'father' but not to 'mother'). The second is a missing relationship (e.g. if the relationship between engine and carriage were to be omitted from Figure 7.4). The first interpretation for 'other than' is that the relationship given is incorrect (e.g. if the relationship between engine and carriage in Figure 7.4 had been given as 'engine is part of carriage' and 'carriage contains engine').

(b)   State Transition Diagrams for Object Oriented Analysis

A separate state model is built for every object and relationship that has dynamic behaviour. The Shlaer-Mellor approach uses a state model in which the actions are accomplished when an instance of an object arrives in a state, rather than being associated with the transition between states. A HAZOP will explore deviations of the attributes of the actions as well as of the events. These are the same attributes as described in Section 7.4.2, and the choice of guide words and interpretations is the same as described in Sections 7.4.2 and 7.4.3.

(c)   Object Communication Model

To provide coordinated behaviour between the objects, the state models communicate with each other via events. The object communication model is used to depict this communication and it shows the asynchronous communication between state models of objects in the system.

As an example we can show, in Figure 7.5, a part of the object communication model for the carriage object and door object of Figure 7.4. Each state model is represented by an oval labelled with the name of the state model. An event generated by one state model or external entity and received by another is shown by an arrow from the generating component (here 'carriage') to the receiver (here 'door'), annotated with the event label (here 'D1'), the meaning of the event (here 'open door') and (optionally) any data associated with the event (here the identification number of the door 'door ID').

In the object communication model, the interaction between objects is defined by the attribute 'event', and this can be the subject of a HAZOP. The choice of guide words and their interpretation in this context is the same as described in Sections 7.4.2 and 7.4.3.

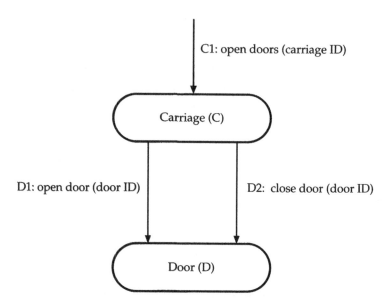

Figure 7.5: Example communication model for part of a train

(d)   *Object Access Model*

In an object oriented system, all processing is within the actions of the state models. These actions are usually defined in terms of processes and object data stores (matching the data attributes of the objects on the entity relationship diagram) and so they are similar to low-level data flow diagrams (see Section 7.4.1).

Processes in an action may need access to the data of other objects as well as the data of the object in whose state model they are embedded. This inter-object data access is shown by an object access model. Thus, while the object communication model shows the asynchronous communication between objects, the object access model gives a summary of the synchronous communication between state models and the data of objects.

When a state model accesses the data of an instance of another object through an accessing process, the data access takes place during the time that the action is running. As an example we show, in Figure 7.6, a small part of an object access model for the train. An object is represented by a flattened oval labelled with the name of the object. The oval represents both the data describing the instances of the object and the state model.

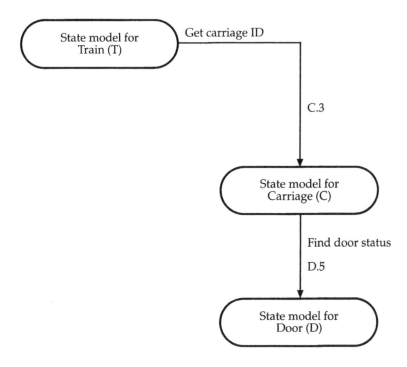

Figure 7.6: Object access model for part of a train

In Figure 7.6, the Train state model needs to access the Carriage ID data in the Carriage state model and the label C.3 gives the identifier of the process within the Carriage state model that will supply the data. Also, the Carriage state model needs to assess the door status data in the Door state model, and the label D.5 gives the identity of the process within the Door state model that will supply the data.

Because the model gives the data flows between the state models a HAZOP can treat each interaction as a data flow. Thus the attribute of interest is 'data flow' and the interpretations are the same as described in Section 7.4.1.

7.4.5 Attributes and Guide Word Interpretations for Digital Electronics

A safety analysis must address all parts of a system, for example the hardware, the software that runs on it, and other associated digital electronics such as sensors and actuators. In this sub-section we give some pointers to how to approach the selection of attributes and guide words for digital electronics.

To show the principles, a simple example of an electrical connection between two component parts of an electrical design is used. For the purpose of addressing interactions between the parts, it does not matter if these parts are discrete components or complex digital systems — the principles are the same.

The attributes selected are listed below with a brief summary of the issues which their choice seeks to address:

- The relationship between the ground (0V) potentials of the two parts ('voltage difference between grounds'). On a connection between discrete components on a printed circuit board with a ground plane this is not an issue. However, it becomes important in systems with, for example, separate ground regimes, large physical separation, or high data rates.
- The physical connection attribute looks at the 'number of connections'. Possible deviations include the possibility of wrong connection and the likelihood and effects of crosstalk and shorting between carriers.
- The two voltage and current attributes ('voltage drive vs loading' and 'current drive vs loading') compare the drive capability of one end with the loading and impact requirements of the other.
- The protocol attributes are 'bi-directional signals' which define the end which may drive the link for bi-directional signals, and 'timing relative to a reference' which, not surprisingly, addresses how the signal is transferred relative to a timing reference.
- The capability of the carrier is explored through the 'wire capability' attribute.

Table 7.4 gives a matrix of those attributes with sample guide word interpretations. In this and the following two tables, the first row contains a reminder of the generic meanings of the HAZOP guide words as an aid to the reader (this row would not normally be included in an attribute-guide-word interpretation matrix).

Table 7.4: Matrix of example attributes and guide word interpretations for digital hardware

	No	More	Less	As well as	Part of	Reverse	Other than	Early	Late	Before	After
Generic meanings	no part of the intention is achieved	a quantitative increase	a quantitative decrease	all design intent but with additional results	only some of the intention is achieved	the logical opposite of the intention	result other than original intention is achieved	relative to clock time	relative to clock time	related to order or sequence	related to order or sequence
Voltage difference between grounds	undefined	too high a difference					grounds thought to be static are moving				
Number of connections	missing or broken connection	not an issue	less connections than signals needed	crosstalk		twisted bus over (0-15)->(15-0)	shorting				
Voltage drive vs loading	too high a difference	over voltage	under voltage			inverted logic (i.e. in the opposite range)	outside valid range but not sufficient to cause change				
Current drive vs loading	no signal	excessive current	insufficient drive or load			current in the reverse direction	outside defined range of currents				
Bi-directional signals	no drive at all hence no signal			more than one output			the incorrect output driving				
Timing relative to a reference	missing reference							relative to clock time	relative to clock time	related to order or sequence	related to order or sequence
Wire capability	missing or broken wire	too high voltage or too high current	too low a current	interference or EMI		acting as a transmission line	wrong wire leading to wrong signals at far end				

Table 7.5: Matrix of example attributes and guide word interpretations for communication systems

	No	More	Less	As well as	Part of	Reverse	Other than	Early	Late	Before	After
Generic meanings	no part of the intention is achieved	a quantitative increase	a quantitative decrease	all design intent but with additional results	only some of the intention is achieved	the logical opposite of the intention	result other than original intention is achieved	relative to clock time	relative to clock time	related to order or sequence	related to order or sequence
Physical topology		there are more nodes than required	there are fewer nodes than anticipated or required		ability to transmit or receive but not both, e.g. duplex becomes simplex		rogue node misbehaving or wrong architecture				
Master	no master node is defined	more active masters than planned	fewer masters active than planned				master is other than the one expected to be in control				
Encoding for reliability	encoding missing	greater reliability at lower bandwidth	less reliability than required				corruption of the encoding				
Protocol	no protocol implemented			other handshakes or other control signals	partial command or response	transmits when should be receiving or vice versa	protocol signals present but wrong	relative to clock time	relative to clock time	related to order or sequence	related to order or sequence
Bandwidth of signals		more than expected (slower or no response)	less data than expected (faster response)								
Data rate	no data is transferred	data rate is too high	data rate too low	in-appropriate loading of a shared channel							

Table 7.6: Matrix of example attributes and guide word interpretations for electromechanical systems

	No	More	Less	As well as	Part of	Reverse	Other than	Early	Late	Before	After
Generic meanings	no part of the intention is achieved	a quantitative increase	a quantitative decrease	all design intent but with additional results	only some of the intention is achieved	the logical opposite of the intention	result other than original intention is achieved	relative to clock time	relative to clock time	related to order or sequence	related to order or sequence
Torque	no torque appears	higher than expected	lower than expected			torque is reversed	torque is cyclic (fluctuating)				
Load	no load	higher than expected	lower than expected				load is in unexpected direction (fluctuating)				
Speed	no	overspeed	underspeed								
Force	no	more than expected	less than expected				fluctuating in wrong direction				
Temperature	no temp measurement	higher than expected	lower than expected				increasing or decreasing				
Material	complete failure		less of material (wear)	corrosion is present	fatigue		creep or failure				
Containment	complete failure of containment				partial loss of containment						
Torque rate	torque is static	increasing	decreasing				unexpected				
Load rate	load is static	increasing	decreasing				unexpected				
Acceleration	constant speed	increasing	decreasing				unexpected or dynamic				
Change of force	constant force	increasing	decreasing				unexpected or dynamic				
Change of temperature	constant temperature	increasing	decreasing				unexpected				

7.4.6   Attributes and Guide Word Interpretations for Communication Systems

More and more systems are being built with intra-system digital communication. In either a communications network or a specific communications link, there are attributes that need to be examined in a HAZOP, such as the topology of the network, the encoding of the data, and the data rate. A matrix of the most common attributes, with sample guide-word interpretations, is given in Table 7.5, and descriptions of the attributes are as follows.

- The topology of a communication system ('physical topology') describes the connectivity between a set of nodes, and whether a node is a transmitter, a receiver, or both. This topology may range from static, through dynamic due to failure, to fully dynamic where nodes can be freely connected or disconnected.

- Activity on the communications system is controlled by one or more master nodes (attribute 'master'). Networks may have more than one master node in order to increase reliability by redundancy or, for networks like Ethernet, the system may support multi-masters.

- Encoding is used to improve the reliability of the system ('encoding for reliability') by providing error detection or error detection and correction capability.

- The 'protocol' defines how the data is transferred between nodes, for example, whether transmission begins following a request from another node or from an internal event.

- The bandwidth of the system ('bandwidth of signals') is the data capacity. At a simple level, the bandwidth will affect response time, which in turn will vary according to the message priority.

- The 'data rate' is the amount of data passed around the network or across the link per unit time, usually expressed as bits per second (bpi). It is a key attribute for both synchronous (locked to a central clock) or asynchronous communication systems.

7.4.7   Attributes and Guide Word Interpretations for Electromechanical Systems

Frequently PES are included in systems together with electromechanical parts, and a complete HAZOP will need to address those electromechanical aspects. A typical mechanical sub-system might include components such as motors, shafts and gearboxes. In Table 7.6 some sample attributes are given for the mechanical parts of such a system, together with example guide-word interpretations. We have found that this set of attributes has been sufficient for carrying out effective HAZOPs of the systems we have examined, but we do not claim that the list is exhaustive. Nearly all the attributes given have their common meanings. The attribute 'material' signifies the physical material out of which the component part is made. The attribute 'containment' signifies the ability of the component under study to retain its contents.

7.5 CONCLUDING REMARKS

In this chapter we have introduced a number of important points about the use of guide words:

- A guide word is a word or phrase which expresses and defines a specific type of deviation from design intent. The use of guide words helps structure and stimulate the creative process of exploring potential deviations.
- A generic set of guide words, including guide words for timing issues, has been provided. It has been found to be applicable to all types of system, including all PES design representations we have studied.
- It should be possible to carry out a HAZOP on any representation that is both precise and understandable.
- The guide words may be interpreted differently in different industries, at different stages of a system's life cycle, and when applied to different design representations. The study leader should define the interpretation of each of the guide words for each attribute of the entities on the design representations to be studied.
- The guide words are used to help the creative exploration by the HAZOP team members of deviations from design intent. The choice of interpretation must be adequate to allow this creative exploration, and it is important to note that there is no universal 'right' set of interpretations.
- When, rarely, a guide word not originally selected or a new interpretation of a guide word is needed during a study, those parts of the system already examined will need to be reviewed using the new guide word or interpretation.
- The example interpretations given in this chapter are ones that have been found to work on particular HAZOPs, but others are not precluded.

8
Planning a HAZOP Study

The core of a HAZOP is the series of study meetings at which an examination is carried out of the design representations of the system under study. If the meetings are to be efficiently carried out and effective in achieving their purpose, a great deal of advance preparation is needed.

Having been appointed and briefed, the study leader may receive delegated responsibility from the study initiator to plan the study. The support of the study initiator may be needed to a greater or lesser degree, depending on the level of the study leader's experience and authority and the cooperation of proposed team members and their managers. Likewise, the study initiator may pay close attention to the preparation of the HAZOP or wait for assistance to be sought, depending on his or her own personality and style of leadership. In the following sections, the study initiator is only occasionally mentioned, the role having been described in Chapter 5, but he or she may be involved in any or all of the activities discussed, depending on the needs of the study leader.

8.1   THE DESIGN REPRESENTATION

It is the study leader's responsibility to ensure that the design representations are available for the study. This requires liaison with the designer, to confirm not only that the representations are ready on time, but also that their quality has already been assured.

As regards time, it is suggested that the date for delivery to the study leader of the design representations by their designers should be at least two weeks before the date of the first study meeting. To allow too little time increases the risk both of lateness and of quality being compromised by a rush at the last minute.

As regards quality, the importance of a thorough design review prior to the HAZOP is vital. A HAZOP should not be used as a design review. If a design representation is of inferior quality, errors are continually found during the study, and this wastes the time of the entire team — and can divert the team's attention, thus introducing the risk of some hazards not being discovered. The study leader should not normally allow a HAZOP to commence if design reviews and quality inspections of the representations have not already been carried out. Further, if it turns out during the study that a design representation is flawed, the study leader should cease the study, and should not sanction its recommencement until the design has been checked and the design representation corrected and quality-assured. This may at first be thought of as a drastic action, but it is not. If we are serious about achieving safety, we must also be conscious of the need to achieve it cost-effectively. Moreover, we must first achieve quality. An efficient and effective HAZOP can be based only on high-quality representations of the system.

The study leader, with the assistance of the designer, must also decide whether the design representations planned for use in the HAZOP are adequate as a basis for identifying all possible hazards. If they are deemed not to be, one or more further representations would be required. Advice on this is offered in Chapter 4.

8.2   SUPPORTING DOCUMENTATION

Depending on the stage of the system life cycle at which the HAZOP is being carried out, it may be necessary to consider the results of one or more previous studies — which may have been HAZOPs or other types of study, such as FMEA.

The results of earlier studies can inform the study team of what hazards were previously detected in the system. By the time of the current study, steps should normally have been taken to eliminate or mitigate them, so one of the objectives of the present study might be to check whether this has been done. Indeed, in some cases, a HAZOP may be carried out only to check that previously found hazards have been mitigated. Then, not only are the results of the previous studies of practical necessity in carrying out the current HAZOP, but they also define its objectives. Further, if the HAZOP is conducted effectively (in accordance with its objectives) it would be shorter and less expensive than otherwise.

If the results of a previous study are suspect, the present HAZOP may be used for checking them. In such a case, the study is referred to as a 'contrasting study', and the previous results should not be used in planning it or carrying it out.

Whereas it is the study leader's responsibility to determine what previous study results are relevant to the present study, he may delegate to the recorder the task of acquiring them, studying their contents, preparing their use for the HAZOP, and, if necessary, distributing and explaining them to the team members.

8.3   ENTITIES, ATTRIBUTES AND GUIDE WORDS

The basis of each HAZOP meeting is the controlled and directed exploration of one or more design representations. The control is provided by the study leader. The direction is provided by guide words, which were described in detail in Chapter 7. If the study leader is to be effective in controlling the study and the direction is to be appropriate to the system being studied, the preparation needs to include the identification of the attributes to be examined for possible deviations from design intent and the choice of appropriate and applicable guide words. It is recommended that the study leader and designer should together carry out this part of the preparation.

First, the study leader must identify the entities on the design representations. As seen in Chapter 4, these may be components on the representation or something which is flowing between components (for example, a fluid in a process plant, or data in an electronic system). Components are normally represented explicitly, so there should be little difficulty in their identification. Flow entities on the other hand are not always listed, and it may take a great deal of analysis of the representation to identify them all. This is particularly true in the case of programmable systems, in which there can be numerous different data and control flows between two processors or between two software modules in the same system. It is recommended that the entities should be listed — on the design representation itself, if there is space; otherwise on a separate sheet.

Once the entities have been listed, their attributes should be identified, as described in Chapter 4. It is unlikely that there will be space on the design representation for the clear and tidy listing of all attributes alongside their entities, so it is recommended that lists be made on separate sheets. It is important to avoid delays and errors at the HAZOP meetings, so clear and logical references should be made between the separate lists and the entities on the design representation.

Having identified and listed the attributes, the study leader and designer should determine which guide words are appropriate for studying each attribute, as explained in Chapter 7. It should be remembered that in associating guide words with attributes, different interpretations emerge according to the circumstances. Lists of the attribute-guide-word interpretations should be drawn up for use in the study. Again, clear references should be made between the lists and the design representations to facilitate rapid and accurate progress during the study.

8.4 SCHEDULE OF THE STUDY

Perhaps the most difficult aspect of initial HAZOP planning is estimating the number of study meetings required. A number of factors are relevant, including:

- The size of the system, or part of the system, to be studied.
- The information available from previous studies of the system. Knowing the number, identity and complexity of hazards found in the past is a significant aid in planning the current study.
- The defined objectives. If, for example, a study is for the sole objective of establishing the adequacy of countermeasures taken against previously identified hazards, it can be planned more accurately and is likely to be considerably shorter than a HAZOP which, starting from scratch, is intended to identify and analyse all possible hazards.
- The quality of the team members. The rate at which they achieve efficiency in carrying out the study depends on whether their relevant knowledge and their ability to perform the necessary roles are complementary, and whether they are 'team players' or individualists. As discussed in Chapter 6, it is the study leader's

responsibility to select appropriate team members.

- The fluency of the team members in a common language. In some multinational development projects, the 'right' people for the HAZOP roles will not necessarily all claim the language of the study as their first language. In one case, a study in English, with an English study leader, a Japanese designer and a Korean user, took about twice as long as had been estimated for a 'single-language' study.
- The calibre and experience of the study leader. If the study leader is an experienced chairman, the team is likely to become efficiently productive more quickly, superfluous discussion is likely to be less, and planned targets are more likely to be achieved.
- A calculation of the time the study will take, based on the number of attribute-guide-word combinations derived from the design representation and the average time taken per attribute-guide-word within the organisation. Data on HAZOP studies should be recorded, analysed and put to use (see Chapter 16). As a guide, an experienced study leader could expect to complete a HAZOP for a process plant with 30 P&IDs in about twenty 3-hour sessions, with the pace being slow at first and fast at the end.

In addition to the logical factors, there are almost certain to be external pressures applied, for example by the managers of the team members for their early return, and by those financing the study for it to be concluded within a maximum number of meetings.

Taking these factors into account, along with others which the study leader and the study initiator may consider relevant, an estimate of the number of meetings should be made. Then a schedule of the meetings, defining dates and times, must be drawn up. Some practitioners have recommended that HAZOP meetings should be spaced out — for example, no more than three or four in a week — so as to allow busy team members to participate in the study while still attending to their other duties. Superficially this seems attractive, but it is usually impracticable for a number of reasons:

- Maintaining a constant team over many weeks is often impossible owing to other commitments, such as holidays;
- Team momentum is lost when there is too large a gap between meetings, particularly if there has not been a sufficiently long run of meetings to build up momentum in the first place;
- When the optimum team consists of members from several locations (or even countries), the meeting schedule must be planned so as to

minimise the costs of travel and time.

- Project timetables often have only a narrow window between data being ready for the commencement of a HAZOP and the need for the results of the study.

The authors therefore recommend, from experience, that HAZOPs should be scheduled as two 3-hour meetings per day, for up to three days, with a break of at least two days before recommencement (see Section 9.5.2).

8.5 RECORDING STYLE

Recording style will be the subject of Chapter 10. Here it is sufficient to note that during preparation the study leader needs to determine what style is to be employed and instruct the recorder and the other team members as to what it is.

8.6 TEAM SELECTION

The selection of the study team was discussed in detail in Chapter 6. Mentioning it here is a reminder that crucial aspects of the planning for the study are choosing appropriate team members, obtaining the commitment of their managers and confirmation of their availability for the full schedule of meetings, agreeing the details of the study with the proposed team members, and selecting substitute team members in case of emergencies. When these tasks have been carried out, the team members need to be briefed — for which see Section 8.9.

8.7 LOGISTICS FOR THE MEETINGS

In considering the technical aspects of a HAZOP, it is not uncommon for the study leader to neglect the 'simple' accommodation arrangements. Yet, if left until the last minute, they often turn out not to be so simple after all. With only a few days to go, rooms which were available a month in advance have been reserved for other meetings; refreshments which would have been arranged by a methodical study leader are forgotten in the panic to find a room; optimum scheduling of meetings becomes impossible because of the need to compromise on accommodation.

The study leader needs first to plan the entire schedule of meetings in the HAZOP. He then needs to determine an appropriate location and to secure suitable accommodation, giving consideration to the requirements of the team members, the necessary facilities, and the need for privacy and quiet. If refreshments are to be provided, these too need to be ordered. If refreshments are not to be provided, it must be ensured that they are available at or near the chosen venue.

A specification for the requirements of each meeting, including the timing of each requirement, should be delivered in writing to those (for example, caterers) with whom arrangements are being made. It is surprising how many arrangements come to grief because requirements have been given verbally and not documented at the time. Explicitly documenting requirements is the surest way of minimising misunderstandings.

It should be pointed out that while the study leader is responsible for organising meetings, and should always personally (with such assistance as necessary) carry out the planning, making the arrangements may be delegated to other staff, not necessarily otherwise involved in HAZOP. However, the study leader should have a system of checks in place, based on timely feedback, so as to ensure that all arrangements have successfully been put in place.

Here is a general checklist of what may be necessary, but it is the study leader's responsibility to decide what is required on any given occasion.

- Meeting room. The room should be large enough for the table chairs and all other necessary furniture, as well as for team members to walk around.
- Meeting table. The room should contain a table large enough not only for all the team members to be seated at it comfortably, but also for them to spread out their copies of the design representations. When design representations are particularly large, they may need to be spread on the table for common viewing. On some occasions it may be useful to pin a large design representation to the wall, in which case, arrangements should be made for the necessary pins, strings or tape.
- Meeting room furnishings. As well as the meeting table, there should be sufficient chairs for all team members with at least one spare. There should be a table for a projector and a screen for projection, and the available space should be such that team members are not compromised by projection. There should also be a table for refreshments and lunch.
- Lighting. As the room may need to be darkened for projection, there

should be adjustable lighting, or more than one light in the room. The windows should have curtains or blinds which exclude light.

- Meeting room availability. The room should be available from at least one hour before each meeting until at least one hour after the last meeting of the day.
- Projection facilities. If the recorder is to display the HAZOP results in real time, a data projector will be necessary. In any case, there is likely to be a need for an overhead projector, in which case, a screen, blank acetates and suitable marker pens will also be required.
- Other display facilities which may be necessary are:

  — A white board.
  — Marker pens for white board.
  — A white board cleaner.
  — A flip chart.
  — Marker pens for flip chart.

- A suitable number of electricity power points, appropriately located, and a power cord extension for the recorder's computer.
- Blank name cards for the team members.
- Refreshments. Provision of, or access to, refreshments (for example, coffee, tea, fruit juice, water) at convenient times during the meetings should be arranged. In addition, arrangements may need to be made for lunch, either in the meeting room or nearby.
- Access should be arranged to a laser printer and photocopier, for any printouts required during the study and for copying worksheets for distribution to the team.
- Access to the building in which the meeting room is located can be a problem, so regular access should be arranged (including the acquisition of security passes) for the study leader and the recorder, and appropriate access for the other team members.

8.8 DOCUMENTING A PLAN

The results of planning a HAZOP should be documented in the form of a HAZOP plan by the study leader for three principal reasons. The first is to demonstrate to the study initiator that all that should have been done has been done. As the study initiator retains responsibility for the plan, it should be presented for approval and signing off before it is put to any other use.

The second purpose of the plan is to inform the team members in advance of all aspects of the study. The plan should therefore be complete, well structured and clear, with all information being explicit and not reliant on interpretation.

The third purpose of the plan is to provide a compact guide for the study leader personally of all that will be involved in the study.

Guidance on what the plan should include is as follows:

- The scope and objectives of the study, as defined by the study initiator.
- The full schedule of meetings in the HAZOP, with their dates and times.
- The venue of each meeting. If all meetings are to be held in the same venue, this can be defined succinctly, but if changes of venue are to occur, each should be defined explicitly, with attention being drawn to the fact of change.
- The composition of the team. If the composition of the team is to change at some point, or if new members are to be introduced at certain meetings for particular reasons (for example, to obtain certain expertise for the exploration of given parts of the design representations), these changes should be defined and the reasons for them given.
- The role of each team member.
- Information on the system to be studied, such as its purpose, the environment in which it is to operate, the intended credentials of its operators, and a summary of its modes of operation.
- The titles and publication or availability details of any documents on which the study depends or which are relevant to the study.
- The details of the entities identified on the design representation, the attributes of the entities, the guide words to be used to direct the study, and the derived attribute-guide-word interpretations. The study leader should ensure that the sheets on which these are defined can be integrated into a section of the plan.
- Templates of any forms which will be used during the study, with explanations of how they will be used.

8.9   BRIEFING THE STUDY TEAM

If the team members are to have confidence in themselves, in each other, and in the team leader, they need to know exactly what to expect of the study. In recruiting them, the team leader should have verbally briefed each one, but it is important that the details of the study are confirmed in writing. There is almost nothing as demotivating as a lack of information and the feeling that one has been ignored or taken for granted. In order to ensure that all team members are fully briefed in advance of a HAZOP, it is recommended that an organisation should have a standard means of informing them — consisting of a letter of invitation together with a briefing pack.

The briefing pack should contain:

- The HAZOP plan drawn up by the study leader and approved by the study initiator;
- The design representation or representations to be used in the study;
- A brief description of the HAZOP process.

The letter of invitation should consist of no more than one side of A4 paper and should:

- Address a prospective team member by name;
- Invite the person to participate in the study;
- Point out that the study will consist not of a single meeting but of a number of meetings;
- Define the date, time and venue of the first meeting;
- Refer to the section of the HAZOP plan in which the details of the other meetings in the schedule are defined;
- Refer to the sheet in the pack on which the HAZOP process is explained;
- Refer individually to the design representations and the HAZOP plan and invite the team member to read each of them carefully;
- Invite the team member to contact the study leader if he or she is not familiar with the design representation to be used in the study or has any other query or cause for concern;
- Ask the team member to confirm attendance at the full schedule of meetings.

8.10 HAZOP REHEARSAL

Getting off to a good start at the first HAZOP meeting depends on every team member being familiar with the HAZOP process and the design representations to be studied. If even one team member is unfamiliar with either, it may be desirable for a rehearsal HAZOP to be held for training.

The easiest way to organise this, particularly in securing the release of team members, is for the training session to replace what would have been the first meeting (or a part of it) of the study. This option should be adopted if it is difficult (perhaps for geographical reasons) to assemble the team in advance of the planned series of meetings — but then the study plan should show this, and the schedule of study meetings should be extended to ensure that the study itself is not compromised.

It is also possible for a training session to be held in advance of the scheduled meetings. The disadvantage of this is that it may be perceived as being remote from the 'real' HAZOP, and team members or their managers may not consider it essential for them to attend. Of course, one possibility would be for only those team members who need the training to attend. However, bringing the team together to conduct a rehearsal HAZOP, even though it is a contrived study, is an opportunity to begin the team-building process. Given the considerable dependence of the success of HAZOP on team dynamics, this is an opportunity not to be missed, if at all possible.

A useful alternative to the rehearsal HAZOP is for the study leader to commence the first study meeting with a brief overview of the HAZOP process, taking one or two hours, and then to launch into the 'real thing', but pausing periodically to reinforce the key points from the overview.

It is the study leader's responsibility to recognise the need for a training HAZOP and to organise it in the most appropriate way in the circumstances.

8.11 CONCLUDING REMARKS

Any activity of importance requires planning for its smooth running and success. A team activity particularly depends on planning: if a team leader is unsure of what to do, or what to do next, or of how to do it, the time of not one but several people is wasted. Moreover, as time is wasted, the participants loose patience and interest, and the harmony and productivity of the team go into decline.

A HAZOP depends for its efficacy entirely on team dynamics and creativity. To whatever extent these are sub-optimal, so the efficiency of the study is diminished. Careful planning and preparation by the study leader is therefore absolutely crucial to the success of HAZOP. The authors have experienced many studies whose lack of success has been blamed by the study leaders and their managers on the ineffectiveness of the HAZOP method, but which, on investigation, has been clearly attributable to the lack of planning and leadership by the study leaders themselves.

This chapter has offered advice on planning a HAZOP. It has advised on what should be planned, where responsibility should be vested, and how participants should be informed of the plans. Further, it has provided examples and templates on which an organisation can base their own guidelines for planning HAZOP.

9
Conduct of a HAZOP Meeting

The focus of a HAZOP is the examination of one or more representations of the design of the system being studied, and this is carried out in a series of study meetings. Being a team event, and therefore depending for its efficiency on team dynamics, the conduct of the meetings must take account of human interactions. Moreover, because safety is the context of the study, it is important that the design representation be examined meticulously. The purpose of this chapter is to explain how a study meeting should be conducted and how these issues are dealt with.

9.1 STARTING THE STUDY

9.1.1 First Meeting

A HAZOP of any but the smallest and simplest systems will occupy a series of meetings rather than a single meeting. In the same way that a system has a life cycle, so does a team. At the commencement of the first study meeting, a number of individuals come together, and it is normally some time before they compose a productive and harmonised team. Experience shows that at the start (for at least the first couple of meetings) progress can be slow. A study leader needs to recognise this fact and be conscious of the need to develop the team, through its 'formation' stage to the full efficiency of its 'production' stage. The efficiency, and ultimately the success, of the study depends on the study leader's ability to achieve this. To facilitate the development of the team, there are eight tasks which the study leader must perform before commencing the main part of the study. These are listed here and summarised in the checklist of Figure 9.1.

- The first is to examine the meeting room, its furnishings and facilities and their layout, and to ensure that they are as specified and that they meet the requirements of the study. This task should be repeated before the start of every meeting.
- The second is to record the presence of the team members and to introduce them to each other.
- The third is to explain the meeting rules to which the team members are expected to adhere and those to which the meetings themselves will conform (see Section 9.5).
- Fourth, the study leader should review, with the team, the study plan which has previously been sent to them. This is to remind them of the purpose and nature of both the system and the study.

Before the meeting:
Check the meeting room, its furnishings and facilities, and their layout

At the start of the meeting:
Record the presence of the team members
Introduce the team members to each other
Explain the meeting rules
Review the study plan with the team
Review the design representations and their conventions
Review the HAZOP process
Review the entities and attributes on the design representations, and the guide words and attribute-guide-word interpretations to be used
confirm the style of recording

Figure 9.1: A study leader's checklist of pre-meeting activities

- The fifth task is to review the conventions used on the design representations to be studied and to ensure that all team members are familiar with them. If the preparation had been carried out as recommended in Chapter 8, the chance of a team member not being familiar with the type of representation is small. However, when a team member is found not to be familiar with the design representation, an explanation of it should be given before the main study commences. Not to do so is to risk losing the team member's expertise at a time when it may be crucial. (See Section 8.10 for options for the preparation of team members.)

- The sixth task is to make sure that all the team members are not only familiar with the HAZOP process but also with carrying it out on a design representation of the type in hand. As discussed in Chapter 8, a rehearsal may have been carried out as a part of the preparation for the study. However, sometimes this is not possible in advance, and sometimes it is decided that it would be more feasible to use the first study meeting for the rehearsal. There are also times when, although the preparation has been carried out completely, the presence of a new or substitute member at the first meeting necessitates a brief practice session. Such a practice session should ideally be carried out on a design representation of the type to be used in the study, but of a very simple system. If such is not available, a section of the study design representation may be used; but the practice should not be considered to replace that part of the main study, and that section of the representation should be re-studied in its proper place in the sequence of the study.

- The seventh task is to review the entities and attributes expressed on the design representation, the guide words to be used, and the attribute-guide-word interpretations which will be applied during the study. Reasons why any other guide words in the generic list do not need to be used should be given. The attribute-guide-word interpretations are, of course, determined uniquely in the context of the particular system and its representation, as explained in Chapter 7.

- The eighth task of the study leader is to remind the team members of the style of recording (which was defined in the study plan) so that not only the recorder but also the other team members will understand clearly the nature of the documentation to be produced (Chapter 10 discusses the recording options).

9.1.2 Designer's Introduction

Having carried out the pre-study tasks, the study leader should ask the designer to explain the system, its purpose, and its environment. This provides the context for the study and facilitates an understanding of the generic and environmentally-based hazards which might affect the system or which the system might cause.

It is also important to define the boundaries of the system and explain the boundaries of the study with respect to the system. This may or may not be done by the designer. In many cases it is more appropriate for the study leader to provide this background, having been involved in the planning of the study. There are times when only some parts of the system are being studied, and it should be clearly stated what part or parts of the system these are. In defining the system boundary, any interfaces and interconnections between the system under study and any other systems, humans, or items of plant, should be identified.

The fifth and sixth tasks in the list in the previous section concern the design representations to be studied. The designer may need to add to what the study leader had done by explaining the representations in the context of the system itself — for example, whether a given design is a logical or physical representation, to scale or not to scale, and so on. The designer should remind the team members of the main principles of the representation, again in the context of the system. For example, if it is a P&ID (piping and instrumentation diagram), it might be explained what chemicals are involved in the flow, how they react when combined, and what the hazardous products are; if it is a finite state machine, the designer might remind the team of what state transitions are; if it is a data flow diagram, he or she might explain that it represents both data and control flows but that it says nothing about their timing. Familiarisation with the design representation engendered by this review can make the study efficient from its commencement.

During the designer's introduction, further relevant and useful information may be added by the user or an expert member — for example, on the operation of the system.

9.1.3 Infrastructure and Environmental Hazards

Hazards may be caused by the failure of components of the system infrastructure (such as the hardware and the operating system of a computer system). Similarly, hazards may arise from damage to or failure of the system owing to natural events in the environment, such as earthquake, tempest, lightning and electromagnetic impulses. All these generic possibilities should be identified and examined, and their results documented, at the start of the first meeting — if they were not identified and studied in a previous study. Thereafter they should not need to be studied again, although a final review at the end of the HAZOP is recommended. The means of studying these issues is the same as that used for the design representation; it is explained in the next section.

9.1.4   Study Leader's Awareness of Human Factors

The team members will be together for many meetings. If any member feels alienated from the process or does not understand it, his or her participation in the study and contribution to it will be significantly reduced and the efficiency of the study will be severely impaired. Thus, the study leader, while maintaining control at all times, must also be alert to the reactions of the team members so as to detect the feedback or body language which suggests boredom, alienation, or reluctance to participate.

9.2   THE STUDY PROCESS

Some or all of the tasks described in Section 9.1 may also need to be performed, at the discretion of the study leader, at the start of any subsequent meeting at which there is a new team member or when a new design representation is introduced into the study. Then, having carried out the introductory tasks and thus set the scene, the study leader commences the study of the design representation.

HAZOP is recognised to be a powerful technique, and its power is based on teamwork and a methodical step-by-step procedure. If short-cuts are taken, there is a risk of compromising the process. In a step-by-step procedure, it is necessary to start at a defined point on the design representation and work in a given direction through it. One recommendation is to proceed from left to right across the representation, or forward from inputs to outputs, choosing entities and interconnections in a logical sequence. However, other modes of operation may also be employed, given that they provide a logical and easily controlled sequence.

The study leader starts the process by selecting an entity on the design representation (see Figure 9.2). He or she marks it and notifies the team members of this starting point. It should be recalled that the entities should

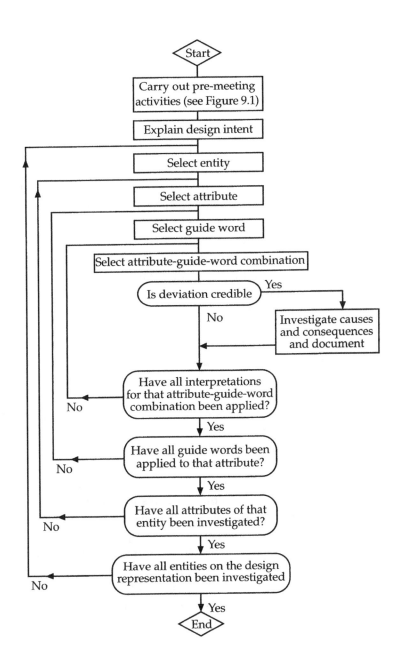

Figure 9.2: Outline of the HAZOP meeting process

have been identified and listed on the representation during the planning of the study. A component is normally a single entity, but an interconnection may comprise a number of entities (for example, a number of chemicals, or a number of data and control flows).

It is essential that all team members are aware at all times of the entity being studied. This may be achieved in several ways, depending on the size of the team and the complexity of the representation — from a single large drawing being pinned to the wall, with the team gathered round it, to each team member having an individual copy and the team leader marking up a transparency copy on an overhead projector.

The purposes of marking what is being studied on the design representation are to keep track of the study and to ensure its completeness. A recommended means of marking is to use one colour of highlighter pen to mark entities (and their attributes, if these are shown on the representation) when their study commences and another colour when it is concluded. Then it is at all times clear what has been studied, what is currently under examination, and what remains to be studied.

Having selected an entity, the study leader's next step is to identify one of its attributes for study. He or she then chooses the first attribute-guide-word combination relating to this attribute (of the selected entity) and announces it to the team. The attribute-guide-word combination, by definition, suggests a deviation of the attribute from its design intent, and the team studies this to see if it is meaningful.

At this point, the relevant results of any previous HAZOPs or other hazard analyses being used to aid the current study may need to be addressed, to see if there are any which are relevant to the attribute under study. (Note that the results of previous studies would not be used if this were a 'contrasting' study, being carried out for the purpose of checking earlier results.) Similarly, if more than one design representation is being used in the study, it may be appropriate to consider the attribute on all of them concurrently rather than in series (see Chapter 12).

The mode of study is as follows. In announcing the attribute-guide-word combination, the study leader implicitly postulates a possible deviation from design intent. Other team members — certainly one or more of the expert members, and possibly others — explore the possibility and consequences of this deviation. In doing so, they may raise questions about its nature, the possibility or likelihood of its occurrence, its causes, and its consequences. In response to the questions raised, explanations may be given by one or more team members, for example, the designer, the user, or an expert member, depending on whether the question relates to the system's design or representation, its operation or operational environment, or other issues. Questions lead to explanations which in turn may lead to further questions and explanations. Thus, a thorough HAZOP depends on creative exploration, team interaction and, ultimately, good leadership.

On some occasions it may be discovered that the design already includes a protection mechanism (that is, a means of ensuring that a fault or failure does not escalate into an accident, for example, an automatic shut-down, or an emergency release valve) or an indication mechanism (that is, a means of warning of the danger of a breach of safety, for example, an alarm). But the presence of either of these should not cause the study to ignore the hazard. The mechanism should be noted as existing, but the hazard should always be thoroughly studied and the results documented. Given the expertise of the team members, their recommendations on countermeasures against a hazard — concerning either the efficacy of existing countermeasures or the desirability of others — may be useful to those responsible for making the system safe. However, they should be documented speedily, for the aim is to identify hazards and not to design or redesign the system. Similarly, risk analysis of discovered hazards should not be carried out during a HAZOP meeting.

Occasionally too, the team may lack essential information. Then the study leader should conclude the discussion by defining the question or questions which need to be answered. The questions should be documented by the recorder for resolution outside the meeting and the study should proceed. Also, if the lack of consensus takes the form of two or more opinions about the system or a hazard, all opinions should be documented by the recorder; they may subsequently aid the design team or others in resolving the problem. A HAZOP is not effective when too much time is spent on discussion. Consensus should be arrived at relatively quickly and it should be rare for one attribute-guide-word combination to be considered for more than ten minutes.

When agreement has been reached on whether or not there is a credible deviation, and what its causes and consequences could be, the study leader concludes the discussion by summarising the results and drawing any relevant conclusions, which are then documented by the recorder. However, occasionally agreement cannot be reached and it is preferable to discontinue the discussion and record the disparate views rather than waste too much time on a single topic. It is at the discretion of the study leader to decide when this time has arrived — but see Section 9.5.1. The study leader should make notes (on the design representation or separately) as an aid to later review and discussion with the recorder. In making notes, we suggest that the study leader mark a numbered reference on the representation, as this helps in identification should doubts arise later in the study.

As a HAZOP should not end on questions, the answers to all questions raised during one meeting must be reviewed in a subsequent meeting of the same study. It may be necessary for the study initiator's authority to be envoked to ensure that timely answers are provided by the appropriate people so that the study schedule is not jeopardised. The study leader should resist the temptation to 'save time' by personally resolving issues between meetings.

When the examination guided by the chosen attribute-guide-word combination has been concluded and its results documented, the next guide word is applied to the same attribute, giving a different attribute-guide-word combination, and the process is repeated (see Figure 9.2). Then, when all attribute-guide-word combinations appropriate to the attribute have been studied, the next attribute of the entity under consideration is chosen and the process repeated. When all the attributes of the entity have been studied, the entity is marked off. Then another entity is chosen and the process repeated.

By thus proceeding methodically, a proportion of the design representation is examined and marked during a meeting.

The postulation of a deviation from design intent (see Section 6.3) depends on a particular design interpretation, and a novel interpretation could lead to a deviation not perceived by the study leader. Should a team member identify a novel design interpretation, the new deviation should be added to the study leader's list and explored. This may necessitate a review of earlier parts of the study.

9.3   RESULTS OF A MEETING

The bulk of the documentation at the end of a study meeting should consist of the details of the hazards discovered and, if full recording is being carried out, of the activities of the study (see Chapter 10). However, there will almost certainly be other results, consisting of conclusions, recommendations, and questions.

Conclusions (which should always be treated as preliminary) may be drawn if there is sufficient confidence to make statements about some aspect of the system and its safety. For example, it may in some cases be possible to conclude that there is adequate protection against a given hazard, perhaps because of countermeasures already in place or of its minimal consequences. Although it is not the purpose of a HAZOP to decide when the design is adequate, if the appropriate experts are together for the study, their opinion may usefully be taken and recorded. Conclusions should, however, formally be reviewed after the end of the meeting.

Similarly, if the assembled experts can make a recommendation on the safety or design of the system, without diverting too much time from the identification of hazards, it may be of help to the system designers later. Recommendations may be for checking existing, or adding further, countermeasures in respect of a named hazard or its cause, for a particular design change, for amending operational procedures, or even for carrying out a further, more detailed study (perhaps an FMEA) of an element of the system. But it should be clear that recommendations are in fact suggestions which may later be amended or even formally rejected by the persons responsible for analysing or implementing them.

While a HAZOP should not end on a question, as this would imply that the study is incomplete, a study meeting can. Questions are documented for resolution outside the meeting when uncertainties which arise during the study cannot be resolved. For example, if the designer is unable to explain the function of an apparently crucial component, or if the user is unsure about the consequence of a deviation from design intent (such as a rise in temperature, or certain data arriving late at its destination), questions would be raised for later resolution.

9.4   THE END OF A STUDY MEETING

At the end of a study meeting, the study leader is responsible for ensuring that the documentation is complete, that it is agreed by the team members, and that it is signed off.

In most cases, the end of a study meeting is not the end of the HAZOP. However, the documentation of each meeting needs to be self-contained, verified by the team members, and signed off by the study leader. The recorder therefore needs to complete the meeting documentation either during or shortly after the meeting, according to the defined recording procedure (see Chapter 10). As follow-up work needs to be carried out and its results presented to a future meeting in the same study, there should be minimal delay in preparing the documentation.

9.5   MEETING RULES

HAZOP is a team study and depends on the team members cooperating and interacting together harmoniously. As, typically, total cooperation does not naturally endure for more than a few minutes, often because a number of people wish to speak at the same time, the study leader has a responsibility to keep order if efficiency is to be maintained. Having a list of rules to which team members know that they are expected to adhere has two great advantages: it provides a basis for the maintenance of order, and it aids the study leader by making it clear that he is not employing arbitrary rules. We therefore recommend that an organisation carrying out HAZOPs should develop a set of rules. The following are guidelines on what they should cover.

9.5.1   Guidance on Control

The following are recommended for controlling a meeting and maintaining progress:

- Whereas everyone who has something constructive to say on a subject should have their say, only one person should speak at a time.
- Extraneous discussion wastes time and reduces the efficiency of the process, so every speaker should be brief and to the point.
- Normally the maximum time spent on discussing a single point should be 10 minutes. In rare instances, the study leader may decide that it is useful to allow continued discussion, but then a maximum of 20 minutes should be observed.
- It is not difficult for the process to become ineffective, for example because the discussion has become unproductive, or some members have been excluded from it and become bored, or if one or more team members have become tired. The study leader needs to be alert to this possibility, and if the meeting appears to have become ineffective he or she should stop it, or declare a break.
- If the study leader recognises that he or she has become ineffective owing to mental overload, the study meeting should be stopped.

9.5.2   Guidance on Efficiency

HAZOP depends on continued concentration, and if the concentration of the team members (including the study leader) lapses, efficiency is lost. It is therefore as well to recognise that alertness and concentration diminish with time and that the duration and scheduling of meetings should be planned to avoid, as far as possible, the resulting inefficiencies. The following are suggestions on which to base meeting rules.

- The duration of a single meeting should not exceed 3 hours.
- At the end of each hour during a meeting there should be a break of about 5 minutes. The study leader should encourage all team members to get out of their chairs and walk around during this break. This improves blood circulation, wakens the sleepy, revives concentration and alertness, and brings new life to the meeting.
- There should not be more than two meetings in any one day.
- There should be an interval of at least 1.5 hours between meetings on the same day.
- When two meetings are being held on the same day, this should continue for a maximum of 3 days. After this there should be a break of at least 2 days before a further meeting is held.

It is recognised that it is costly to keep a HAZOP team together. Economic considerations should therefore be taken into account in advance when planning the meeting schedule and not used later as an excuse for not observing the defined meeting rules. If the best results are desired, it is important that account be taken of the need for continued alertness and concentration.

9.6   CONTROL OF THE MEETING

A HAZOP is only as good as the team taking part. Like most team activities, the personal knowledge and skill of the team members are important to success. The way the team members work together is crucial. One of the advantages of the process is that the team can build on a comment by any team member and explore unusual interactions on the design representations. A HAZOP is therefore a creative activity. In order for creative resonance to be achieved, the study leader's control and leadership are vital.

The study leader, therefore, needs not only to be a firm chairman but also someone who understands team dynamics. He or she needs to be capable of knitting the team into a unit, developing it rapidly to efficient productivity, maintaining it in a harmonious mode of operation, detecting embryonic problems, and resolving them before they materialize. As a last resort, the study leader should have the authority, indeed the responsibility to the team, to stop a meeting at any time if it is not productive, and to take action to control (including the possibility of expelling) a team member who is not contributing, who is being disruptive, or who is otherwise obstructing the smooth working of the team or in any way compromising the effectiveness or efficiency of the meeting.

9.7 HAZOP TOOLS

Numerous tools exist to aid the conduct of HAZOPs. They range from simple paper to complex software packages. While this book focuses on the principles of the HAZOP process, it is worthwhile mentioning the availability of tools.

First, it is possible to acquire basic computer-based HAZOP tools, consisting mainly of formatted pages, which can help the team leader to conduct the study and the recorder to document the results. They enable the study leader to create a tailored list of attributes, guide words, and attribute-guide-word interpretations, and to use it to ensure consistency during the study. They allow the results to be documented in columns and, in some cases, alternative formats, and to be recorded on-line, enabling the team to review (and edit) them at the end of the study. They also allow their rapid printing and, therefore, off-line editing when this is necessary.

More sophisticated tools facilitate the creation of one-to-one and one-to-many relationships between attributes, guide words, and attribute-guide-word interpretations, so that when the study selects an attribute, only the relevant or meaningful guide words and attribute-guide-word interpretations are applied to it. These tools also provide a protection facility by preventing the progress of the study until all attributes, guide words, and attribute-guide-word interpretations have been applied. This ensures completeness of the study as well as full recording not only of the results but also of the proceedings. In addition, they can provide for the recording of attendance at the HAZOP meetings.

While being useful aids to the control and recording of a HAZOP, such tools do not replace the team-based investigation which is the core of the process. The benefits that they offer are in speeding up the recording process and in helping to ensure completeness and consistency in the study and the documentation of its results.

However, in the chemical industry, attempts have been made to develop tools to automate the HAZOP process itself. They enable the development of a software-based description of the system which is then subjected to a form of automatic HAZOP. The results of this are then made available to the study team who can check them and add items when necessary. The advantage of such tools is that they substantially accelerate the study and reduce the effort required from the study team. However, as they are incapable of detecting the hazards inherent in a chemical process, the knowledge required to do so must be entered separately. In some 'expert system' tools, this is done as a set of expert rules. In other tools, it may be provided as the results of an FMEA on the system components. For example, if an FMEA revealed that 'pressure-more' in the reactor could lead to a run-away reaction, and explosion if the pressure were to exceed a certain value, and this information were entered, the tool would search for the possible causes of 'pressure-more' using the HAZOP technique. Similarly, if all the failure modes were entered into the tool, it would repeat the process for them. Whether the tool is based on an expert system or on the processing of FMEA results, it is only as good as the information provided on the system's hazards, and it must be ensured that this is complete if confidence is to be placed in an automatic HAZOP.

Like any tool, HAZOP tools need to be used within their limits, and we believe that care should be taken in their application. They cannot fully cover all the nuances of the HAZOP process and so may reduce or even destroy a study team's imaginative investigation of a system. If used by a team which employs a creative approach, as advocated in this book, with the tool used to generate a check list of what should be covered, or to facilitate the recording of the results, or to provide initial assessments of possible causes and consequences, then they can be of value. But if they are used to reduce the HAZOP to a quick review of the tool's results by a small team, or even by a single person, we feel that the resulting process could not be classified as a HAZOP in the sense accepted in this book.

10
Recording, Signing-off and Follow-up Work

During a HAZOP meeting, the recorder documents the results of the study according to the style defined in the objectives set by the study initiator. At the end of each meeting the study leader must sign-off the documented results as being a faithful record. Subsequently, the results of follow-up work may need to be fed back to a later meeting in the same HAZOP study. This chapter explains the processes of recording and signing-off the results of a meeting and dealing with follow-up work.

10.1   RECORDING

10.1.1   The Need to Record

The results of a HAZOP need to be recorded for future use. Not only may the results of a study be used as the input to later stages of safety analysis of the system, including later HAZOPs, but also the results of a particular meeting may be necessary to later meetings in the same study. Any hazards found also need to be documented in the system or project 'hazard log' subsequent to the study. As the results are so important, their immediate documentation should be well structured and their details clear and unambiguous. It is recommended that:

- Standard forms should be designed to facilitate recording;
- The recorder should be highly competent (see Chapter 6);
- The study leader should monitor recording and ensure that it is done on the standard forms, that it is tidy, that it adheres to the standards laid down, and that the results of the study are fully and clearly documented and understandable;
- HAZOP results should be capable of being subjected to independent audits, which might be carried out from time to time.

In planning a HAZOP, it needs to be decided what style of recording will be employed: should all activities during the study be recorded, or only those which result in the identification of hazards? The answer should be provided by the study initiator at the time of defining the scope and objectives of the study.

10.1.2   Recording Style

Currently, there are two recording styles in use. The first is to document every study activity and the second is to record exceptions only — that is, activities which result in the identification of a hazard, questions which cannot be answered at the meeting, or recommendations.

(a)   Full Recording

When the full recording style is employed, the application of every attribute-guide-word interpretation is documented. In each case a deviation from design intent is proposed, and it and all its possible causes and consequences are listed. Some deviations may suggest a hazard, while many (often most) are likely to be considered benign, so the recording can be repetitive.

One means of minimising the tedium produced by this repetition, on both the recorder and the other team members, is to employ prepared recording forms which contain the attribute-guide-word interpretations to be used in the study; the lists made by the study leader in planning the study can be used in preparing the forms. Another means of minimising the work is to use an electronic tool — see Section 9.7. In any case, the recorder must ensure that recording is carried out efficiently and that no trace of its difficulties or tedium is allowed to affect the other team members.

The full recording style provides a complete record of all that transpired at the HAZOP, and this offers a number of advantages:

- It is available to the study initiator, other management, and those responsible for the certification of the system, for verifying that the study was carried out according to its plan and that it met its objectives;
- The record provides a full description of all deviations considered, and so should meet the requirements of quality and safety auditors;
- It provides evidence of what was done at the HAZOP to an enquiry into any later system failure or breach of safety. In the event of litigation, it can be of considerable advantage to be able to demonstrate the full coverage of the HAZOP.

Full recording produces a complete and auditable set of results, but there is a chance that if the potential tedium is not alleviated, the team will become less motivated and creative than otherwise. Thus, full recording requires the study leader to plan the study carefully, to be extremely well prepared, and to be creative in leadership of the study.

(b)   Exception Recording

Exception recording leads to less, and therefore more manageable, documentation, and this can be a great advantage when it comes to obtaining the team's agreement to what has been documented. Further, given the degree of repetition likely in full recording, exception recording is not likely to diminish the value of the study or to mitigate against the study's objectives being met. However, it does not document the full extent of the activities carried out during the study and thus does not provide evidence of thoroughness. It is therefore less likely to satisfy the full criteria of quality or safety auditors. Moreover, its failure to provide evidence of thoroughness makes it less useful as defence against a liability suit. In these days of increasing litigation, this may be considered relevant in some cases.

In the 1970s, exception recording was the norm, but by the early 1990s it had itself become the exception.

(c) Selecting a Style

In initiating a HAZOP, the study initiator must decide which recording style is to be used. In some cases, particularly when the study is to be carried out on behalf of a third party or when it must conform to predetermined rules within an organisation, the choice may already be defined. In other cases, such as when a contrasting study is to be carried out for the purpose only of checking the results of a previous study, or for verifying that previously identified hazards have been eliminated or adequately mitigated, it may be clear that exception reporting would suffice.

But, generally, in setting the objectives for the study, the study initiator needs to consider the potential trade-off between full and exception recording. A number of other factors may influence the study initiator's decision, including the following.

- Any regulatory requirements which must be satisfied in carrying out the HAZOP. Regulation may arise because of the industry sector in which the system is being developed or used, or because of the need for assessment or licensing of the system.
- Any requirements included in standards which are in use with respect to the system. International, national, industry or company standards may be used within the company developing or operating the system, with the implication (or mandate) that their terms must be observed.
- Auditing requirements. An audit of the HAZOP process may be carried out within the organisation, by independent assessors, or by a client organisation.
- Whether the organisation has a policy on the style of recording to be used.
- The contractual agreement with a client. Whatever the policy or custom of the organisation carrying out the HAZOP, it may need to be overridden by an obligation demanded or implied in a contractual agreement.
- Exception recording is normally a great deal less expensive, as it takes considerably less time.

10.1.3   What is to be Recorded

It was shown in Chapter 3 that there are three types of output from a HAZOP, the hazards identified, questions raised during the study, and recommendations made (usually to carry out an activity, such as a further study into some issue, or, more rarely, to make a change to the design of the system). Whichever recording style is employed (full or exception only), the following (as a minimum) should be observed:

- Recording should be done on predesigned forms (which may be on an electronic medium or on paper). This facilitates both auditing of the HAZOP documentation and later use of the results.
- A different identifier should be used for each of the types of output. For example, a hazard found might be indicated by 'H', a recommendation by 'R', and a question by 'Q'. This facilitates the identification of actions to be taken, both short-term actions necessary to the continuation of the HAZOP and long-term actions for the safety of the system.
- There should be a numbering system such that each type of output is distinguishable and each item is uniquely identifiable. This facilitates the traceability of items, the identification of resulting actions, the checking of follow-up work, and later auditing.

The three types of output are considered in more detail in the following paragraphs.

(a)   Identified Hazards

Each identified hazard must be recorded as an individual entry so as to avoid ambiguity. In some studies it is found that the same hazard recurs as the result of a number of attribute-guide-word interpretations. Then, although each recurrence should still be separately recorded against the appropriate entity and attribute, the details may be documented in one record only, with a reference being made to it from each of the others. Similarly, a recommendation about the hazard might be made only once. However, if the same hazard arises in different entities, beware of concluding too hastily that its cause, or the recommendation to be made, is the same in each case. Certainly, recommendations based on assumptions about the design should be made only with great care.

When a hazard is identified, it is not uncommon for the designer present to claim that it would be impossible for the hazard to materialize into an accident because of some aspect of the design which has been included as protection against it, or because of an alarm which would alert operators to its imminence. To ignore the hazard on these grounds would be to assume that the countermeasure is perfect. The hazard should never be ignored or assumed to be impossible. As advised in Chapter 9, it should be recorded, and on recording forms there should be a column provided for information on 'protection or mitigation' mechanisms. If appropriate, a note may also be added regarding the team's opinion of whether the countermeasure is adequate.

(b) Questions Raised

For every proposed deviation from design intent during a HAZOP, there should be a conclusion that the deviation is either hazardous or not hazardous. If there is doubt, the team can neither conclude with a recommendation on an identified hazard nor dismiss the likelihood of a hazard. Then a question needs to be raised, recorded and subsequently answered, and the answer used at a later study meeting (or, sometimes, between meetings) to resolve the doubt and achieve a conclusion regarding the deviation.

Examples of causes of doubt are:

- The designer is uncertain about some aspect of the design;
- The designer and user are unable to resolve a question on the response of the design or the system to given stimuli, signals, or actions of an operator;
- The user is unsure about the effect that a given system output would have on the environment;
- The user is unable to provide information on one or more aspects of operation.

It is important for the answers to questions to be immediately interpretable by the study team, so the phrasing of questions by the study leader should not be casually done. In general, it is good policy to phrase questions so as to ask directly if something is 'OK'. For example, 'Is the manual valve V-23 readily accessible from ground level?' Then, only if the answer is other than 'yes' does the study team need to debate the issue.

A HAZOP cannot be concluded with questions unanswered. Thus, the recording procedure needs to ensure not only that each question is well defined, but also that the team member or other person responsible for resolving it is identified and a date is set by which the answer is provided to the study leader. Documentation should include both the responsible person's identity and the target date for the question's resolution.

While a nominated team member may not personally be capable of researching the answer to the question, he or she becomes responsible to the study for ensuring that it is answered, that the answer is complete and well defined, and that the answer is delivered to the study leader on time.

(c)   Recommendations

Normally a recommendation is made for carrying out further study into some issue. Examples of when recommendations may be made are:

- If a hazard has been identified but its effect or cause is uncertain, a recommendation for an appropriate study may be made. In this case, the continuation of the HAZOP would not be dependent on the result of the recommended study, so there would be no need for it to be reported back to the study leader before the end of the study.
- If the study of a deviation from design intent shows that there is no hazard but reveals an inadequacy in the design, a recommendation may be made to review and improve that part of the design.
- A recommendation may relate to a later phase of the system's life cycle or of the development project. For example, it might say, 'Ensure that operating procedures specify that ...'.

A HAZOP meeting should not be used for designing or redesigning a system. Nor, for reasons already given, should it be a forum for extended discussion on countermeasures which may be taken against hazards. At the same time, it should be recognised that the team is (or should be) a gathering of experts, and to them it may in some cases be immediately obvious what actions might usefully be taken as a result of one or more findings of the study. It may therefore, when the team members agree on a countermeasure to a particular hazard, be appropriate to recommend its implementation. It should be noted, however, that this should not commit the designers to taking the recommended action. Always recommendations should be investigated thoroughly subsequent to the HAZOP.

10.2   SIGNING-OFF

There are two aspects of signing-off which need to be considered, the signing-off of each study meeting and that of the HAZOP itself. The former is the responsibility of the study leader and the latter of the study initiator.

10.2.1   Signing-off a Study Meeting

The onus is on the study leader to satisfy himself that the recorder's documentation is a faithful record of the meeting, in the defined recording style, and then to sign it off as such. It is also important, however, that the rest of the study team should approve the records, and this can add significantly to the work of the study team.

(a)   *Presentation of the Documentation to the Study Team*

Whether a paper-based or electronic recording system is used will influence the manner in which the recorded documentation can be presented to the study team. The following are examples of the possibilities.

- Most often, whatever the recording medium, the study leader will, after an item has been studied, summarise the result for the agreement of the team and for documentation by the recorder. If the recorder has already documented the item, the study leader's summary will be used for checking.
- It is also possible for the recorder to read the documented results aloud to the study team, item by item, either after each entity has been investigated or at the end of the meeting, thus providing the study team with the opportunity to correct any misinterpretations made by the recorder. But experience shows that many team members do not listen and the time is wasted, so it is not recommended.
- When an electronic means of recording is used, it may be possible to arrange to project the documented results on to a screen as soon as they have been recorded — or at the end of the meeting. However, such visibility can lead to numerous requests for trivial editing, and this can be time-consuming.
- The study leader and recorder can use the night between study meetings to check and edit the documentation produced in the one or two meetings held in a given day. (Note that using the time between two study meetings in the same day for this purpose is too onerous a task. The study leader must remain alert at all times during meetings and should not succumb to the temptation to use the lunch break for this.) On the next day, the updated documentation is presented to the team members for their approval. The preferred method of doing this is by overhead projector, as the study leader can control the pace of the presentation and the amount of paper used is limited. Something to beware of is that there is the possibility of a change in the team, and this can result either in a member of the previous day's team being absent during the review or in the time of a new member being wasted. Further, when the documentation is from the last meeting of a series, an extra meeting would need to be convened in order for such a review to be carried out. If paper is

used instead of overhead projection, there is the possibility for the team members to study it in their own time subsequently, but this necessitates the copying of a great deal of paper and it means that the study leader has the added task of coordinating the responses later.

It should be noted that for the first three methods mentioned above the study leader will not have checked the documentation prior to its presentation to the study team. If any of them is used, the leader must be capable of making a check quickly so as not to be distracted for too long from the sometimes difficult task of controlling the meeting. The attention of the other team members depends critically on the study leader, and it rapidly wanes if there are frequent pauses owing to the leader's own inattention or if the meeting becomes bogged down in superfluous discussion.

(b)   Agreement of the Study Team

The agreement of all the team members to the documentation is necessary, and it is the study leader's responsibility to obtain it. Experience suggests that it is preferable to carry out the document review and gain agreement at the meeting in which the documentation is produced. This makes a number of demands on the study, for example:

- The study leader must allow time for reviewing the documentation in the planning of the meetings and their schedule;
- The recorder must be experienced, expert, and able rapidly to interpret the results of each discussion into clear, understandable prose;
- An electronic recording tool is, ideally, necessary;
- The study leader must control meetings such that reaching agreement does not take an inordinate amount of time.

It may reasonably be expected that on most occasions, given a good recorder, agreement will be easily reached. There are times, however, when consensus is difficult to achieve. Then, the study leader may need to discontinue discussion, instruct the recorder to record the different opinions expressed on the point at issue, and proceed with the review. It is seldom of value to allow discussion for more than a few minutes on a single point during the review of the documentation.

The study leader should be particularly careful to ensure that team members responsible for carrying out follow-up work are reminded of this during the documentation review and that they reiterate their agreement both to do the work and to report the results to the study leader by the defined completion date. A copy of the relevant worksheet of the documentation should then be copied to the team member responsible for a given action. Here, an electronic means of recording offers an advantage in that sorting the meeting's results may be carried out easily and quickly.

(c)   Signing the Documentation

Although an electronic medium is suitable for both documenting the study results and gaining the team's agreement to them, a paper copy is essential for signing-off by the study leader. Proper, auditable, signing-off requires that the pages are numbered and that each page is individually signed by the study leader.

10.2.2   Signing-off a HAZOP

Has the HAZOP been completed? Has each study meeting been thorough? Has the study met its objectives and remained within its defined scope? Has the documentation been produced according to the prescribed style? Is it understandable, and are all identified hazards clearly defined? The study leader has signed-off each study meeting, but this was done without consideration of the HAZOP as a whole. Now the study initiator, who initiated the study and set its objectives, needs to review the results and sign it off.

The study initiator's review should be completed within a short time of the final study meeting, so as to be able to keep the study team together if deficiencies need to be rectified before the HAZOP can be signed-off. This implies that towards the end of the study schedule the study leader should invite the study initiator to begin reviewing the documentation.

10.3   FOLLOW-UP WORK

Follow-up work from a meeting may be considered to consist of dealing with both the questions and the recommendations arising from that meeting. However, while the questions must be answered before the HAZOP can be concluded, this is not necessarily so with the recommendations. The studies which are the subjects of the recommendations may be carried out after the HAZOP study has been completed; whether they have been completed may be an issue for a later HAZOP, or for a subsequent part of the continuing hazard or safety analysis of the system in question, but it may not need to detain the current study. However, it should be noted that the distinction between a question and a recommendation may not be great and in some cases it may be determined by the wording used by the study leader or the recorder. For example, a question may be worded as, 'Is the mitigation adequate?' whereas a recommendation may be worded as 'Check that the mitigation is adequate.'

The study team members with actions to resolve questions should report their results to the study leader by the appointed time. Meanwhile, the study leader should maintain a list of outstanding questions and keep in touch with the persons responsible for them so as to ensure timely resolution.

When the results of a question become available, the study leader should review them and plan their presentation and use at a subsequent study meeting. The study leader has the responsibility to ensure that the study documentation is updated with the new information, with details of its origin, and with its impact on the study, so the recorder must always be involved. Then the resulting study output needs to be signed off by the study leader, with the approval of the study team.

When the new information is used at a study meeting, the part of the system to which the question applied must be re-introduced to the study. In most cases the review in the light of the new information would be expected to be brief, and the current study team would deal with it, with the result being documented as part of the previously scheduled meeting. However, in extreme cases, the study leader may need to make plans for the appropriate team members, particularly the relevant designer, to be present.

When there are several questions whose answers are likely to require the attention of the study team, it may be appropriate for the study leader to schedule a follow-up meeting especially for dealing with the feedback from the follow-up work. When questions are raised at or near the final meeting in a study schedule, such a follow-up meeting becomes even more likely.

10.4   CONCLUDING REMARKS

The detail, structure and accuracy of documentation is critical, because a HAZOP has a number of important influences: it has a crucial impact on the evolving safety of the system under study, it influences (and may even determine) the subsequent studies to be carried out to achieve or investigate the safety of the system, and it may have a similar influence on other future safety analysis activities.

This chapter has offered advice on the style and content of study documentation, as well as on the way in which follow-up work and its results should be handled.

11
Hazard Identification Throughout the Life of a System

The identification and the subsequent analysis of hazards are activities that should be repeated and refined a number of times during the life of the system. In this chapter we review the role of hazard identification during the life of a system so as to provide a context for HAZOP.

As described in Chapter 2, HAZOP is just one of a number of techniques for the identification of hazards, their causes and consequences. In general, the choice of which technique to use is difficult, and little guidance exists on making it. In this chapter we describe the approach we use to choose the most appropriate technique for each of the studies carried out during the various stages of the system's life cycle. We also compare HAZOP with Fault Mode and Effects Analysis (FMEA), an inductive technique that is complementary for identifying hazards and their causes.

11.1 REPEATING HAZARD IDENTIFICATION

The objective of repeating the hazard identification process, within the life cycle described in Section 2.2, is to be as sure as possible that a complete set of relevant hazards and causes is obtained, so that we can ensure that they are correctly managed. As knowledge about the system's design and operation increases, the project team repetitively asks four questions:

- Does the design adequately address the hazards and causes already identified by previous studies?
- Have any new hazards or causes been introduced by changes in the design?
- Does the increased knowledge about the system and its proposed or actual operation enable previously existing but unidentified hazards or causes to be found?
- What extra information can be gained about the potential causes and consequences of the hazards previously identified?

From these questions we can see that repeating the hazard identification process is not just a matter of confirming that the hazards and their causes have been identified. There is also a need to confirm that the correct technical and managerial measures are in place to reduce the risks posed by the hazards to acceptable levels. There is an additional benefit gained, which is that repeated study and confirmation will help to ensure that the hazard set is complete and well understood. This in turn leads to increased confidence in the safety of the system.

It should be made clear that when the hazard identification process is repeated, different techniques may well be used, as discussed below and in Section 2.4.1, and that different representations and levels of design detail will be studied.

11.2 WHY REPEAT HAZARD IDENTIFICATION?

Assuring safety demands a number of activities over the entire life cycle of a system. In managing safety we wish to ensure that we have as complete an understanding as possible of a system's hazards. There are three reasons (described below) why we need to repeat the hazard identification activities, all driven by the fact that hazard and safety analyses can never be considered to be definitive and should be continuously updated throughout the system's life.

11.2.1   Changes During the System's Life Cycle

The first reason for repeating hazard identification is that the hazards of a system will change during the different phases of its life cycle. It is possible to identify three principal phases of hazard identification, each addressing a particular phase of the system's life cycle.

The first phase of studies is done during development, before the system is put into operation. These studies aim to ensure that the system that will initially operate is as safe as necessary. In order to ensure completeness, development hazard identification studies need to be repeated as modifications are made. Because of the nature of developments, modifications normally occur continuously. The hazard identification should be repeated whenever significant milestones in the development process are reached. These might include concept design, basic design, detailed design, first prototype, etc. It is important to remember that the final pre-operational design and construction phases may well involve last minute design changes and thus require similar repeated studies to reflect these changes.

The second phase is during operation itself, when any changes to the system or to its operational environment are analysed to see if the hazards and their causes have changed. It is also useful during this second phase to use the increased knowledge of the system that operation generates. This knowledge is fed back into the hazard identification and safety analysis process, in order to confirm or modify the conclusions of earlier studies.

The third phase of the identification, which is often forgotten and unplanned, covers the decommissioning of the system, during which a series of totally new hazards may exist.

11.2.2   No Hazard Identification is Perfect

The second reason is that hazard identification is not a perfect process and no single study will identify all the system hazards and all their causes and consequences. This is because, like any human activity, hazard identification is subject to error, even if all the necessary information is available. Having additional studies is also a good method of introducing redundancy and further checks into the overall hazard identification process. Repeated hazard identification, particularly during the initial development phase, will help to ensure that as complete a set of well-understood hazards, causes and consequences as possible is identified and analysed.

11.2.3 Availability of Information

The third reason is that the information required for a complete study may not be available when a study is carried out. Hazard identification needs to identify not only the hazards but also their causes. Yet detailed causes cannot be known until a detailed design is available. It is only when the causes of a hazard are known that we can begin to manage the hazard and reduce its probability of occurring. The only exception to this is the rare case where a hazard can be totally eliminated early in the safety analysis process.

Initially the process will focus on identifying hazards, while understanding that their detailed causes cannot be identified until more design detail is available. As the system is designed, more and more design detail will be available. The hazard identification process will then switch from a focus on hazard identification to a focus on cause identification. Finally it will focus on tracking the causes through the different levels of design detail down to the ultimate low-level causes.

11.2.4 Do Not Wait Until it is Too Late

Some have attempted to respond to the three reasons discussed above by delaying the hazard identification until a large amount of design detail is available. This approach is seriously flawed as it results in no safety strategy and planning being developed until the design is nearly complete.

Any development must have early studies that enable the system designers to identify the principal hazards and to understand the nature of the system that they are working on. They should then feed this knowledge into the system safety and design strategies. If this is not done, the system may reach a level of detailed design at which the necessary modifications to ensure safety are costly in both financial and project duration terms.

11.3 WHEN TO REPEAT HAZARD IDENTIFICATION DURING THE LIFE CYCLE

Many hazard identification studies should be carried out during the system's life. Appropriate times, *as a minimum*, include:

- Very early in a system's life, in order to develop a preliminary understanding of the hazards of the system;

- When a high-level design, which captures the main design and operational features, is available;
- During the design process and, as a minimum, when a detailed design is produced;
- When the documentation of the 'as built' system and its operational environment is available;
- After a reasonable period of operation, when significant operational experience is available;
- When changes are to be made, but before they have been implemented on the operational system, or when changes are to be made to the environment in which the system operates;
- Before decommissioning the system.

Three of these (initial hazard identification, when operational experience exists, and decommissioning) are discussed in more detail below, so as to enable the reader to understand the differences between them. Then, in Section 11.4, we discuss the techniques that should be used as the level of design detail increases and the system moves through its life cycle.

It should be noted that we can include in the environment of a system such aspects as the human-machine interface and its respective operating instructions, interfaces with other systems, and external influences such as electromagnetic interference. (See Chapter 13 for more information on modelling and hazard identification where the human-machine interaction is an integral part of the system.)

11.3.1   The Initial Hazard Identification

In the initial stage of safety analysis, the principal aim is to discover whether the system being designed and built has significant safety implications and what hazards it presents. If there are safety implications, any hazards identified at this early stage are used for determining the safety strategy for the system and for planning the number and scope of future studies. Clearly, as there will be a lack of design detail available, one cannot expect such an initial study to be very detailed. However, it is important that the first hazard identification is not delayed too far into the life cycle. There are three main reasons for this:

- *Cost effectiveness* — detailed hazard identification is only likely to be cost-effective when planned from an early higher-level systematic identification of the hazards that has set an overall hazard management strategy;

- *Overall development strategy* — early identification of high-level hazards can help define the overall strategy for system development and operation;
- *Using the most effective hazard identification techniques* — an early study can help identify the types of hazard identification techniques that should be employed in later studies. Each technique is appropriate to the examination of certain types of causes and an early study can help establish future requirements for different methods. Also, if well planned, the different methods used can be complementary.

The technique and approach that is used for the initial hazard identification will depend on a number of factors, and these are discussed in general in Section 11.5, and in particular in Section 11.5.1

The initial hazard identification should be carried out as early as possible in the system's life cycle, for example when the basic design concept has been established. It will then be the basis of the safety management of the system's early development. Subsequently, if the initial design concept changes substantially the hazard identification will need to be repeated, but at least a strategy for doing so will have been defined.

The results of the initial hazard identification and analysis (sometimes called the preliminary hazard analysis or PHA) should be used as an early guide to the hazards of the system. It should, however, be updated later in the system's life cycle unless there has been no change in the basic design concept. This is because the early study will almost certainly be based on and structured around the early design concept. Hazard identification studies are structured around the system design, so the structure of the hazard identification reflects, to quite a high degree, the system's architecture. Thus, an early study will be structured around the initial design concept rather than the final design concept, and trying to force-fit a modified version of the initial study on to the final design concept often causes substantial confusion.

Prior to operation, a number of further hazard identification studies will be required. These are discussed in Sections 11.4 and 11.5, but for now we move on to the operational phase studies.

11.3.2 Experience of Operation — How Does the System Really Behave?

After an initial period, it is almost certain that the system's operation will not be exactly as originally planned. If any substantial changes in operation have occurred, then a further hazard identification study is required.

However, even if the changes have not been substantial, a study that uses the insight gained from operation of the system is beneficial.

Once a first study of the operational system is complete, the need for additional studies should be reviewed regularly. Additional studies will be required before any changes to the operational system, or the environment in which it operates, occur. A brief study should be carried out to review whether the changes could possibly affect the safety of the system in any way. If it is then felt that the changes could have a substantial effect on safety, a series of detailed studies should be planned.

In our experience, such studies should also address the problems of replacing any sub-systems. Two examples are changes to the software within computer-based railway signalling and chemical plant shut-down safety-critical systems. These changes can introduce new hazards that need to be well understood if they are to be managed during the replacement process and, later, during resumed operation. This is especially true if the old and new systems must function in parallel.

11.3.3   Decommissioning

Before decommissioning a system, it is necessary to ensure that the decommissioning process does not introduce any new hazards or change the safety impact or risks associated with the known hazards (i.e. does not introduce a change in the system's hazard profile). It is likely that decommissioning will have a major impact on the hazards of a system and that new or more risky hazards will exist during decommissioning, even if only for a short time.

It is essential that the new hazards and the changes in the known hazards be identified prior to decommissioning. Then their impact on the planned decommissioning should be analysed, as discussed in Sections 11.2.2 and 11.2.3. Based on this analysis the risks associated with the decommissioning should be evaluated so that a safety analysis can be carried out to ensure that decommissioning hazards are also managed. If the risks are too high then measures should be taken to mitigate them.

11.3.4   Managing the Outputs from the Studies

The hazard identification process will at each level of design detail identify those 'components' of the system (hardware, software, firmware, functionality, etc.) that have a role in safety, and ensure that the hazards associated with the different components of the system are identified.

A component which at one level has been shown to have no safety role should not be excluded from future hazard identification, as the earlier identification may later be proved incorrect, but it may justifiably receive less attention.

Once hazards have been identified they should then be analysed and the analysis should form part of the overall safety strategy and plans, as discussed in Chapter 2.

The use of a hazard log is an approach that we have found to be very useful in managing and tracking the outputs from the various studies. It can also allow tracking of the role of the components in the safety of the system. A hazard log is a register of the hazards found and their causes. Usually, it is also used to track planned actions, responsibilities for action, closure of the actions, and finally confirmation that all the hazards and causes identified have been addressed.

11.4 HAZOP AND FMEA

The place of HAZOP in the life cycle process will be discussed in Section 11.5. Prior to this it is useful to consider the differences between HAZOP and a purely inductive technique, such as fault mode and effects analysis (FMEA), and also how they can complement each other. (See Section 2.4.1 for an introduction to FMEA and other hazard identification techniques.) HAZOP and FMEA are frequently confused. Further, when a HAZOP is being carried out, there is normally some element of FMEA of the components of the system included within it. This is not necessarily a bad thing, given that the aim is to identify hazards, but if the difference between the two techniques is understood, their effectiveness can be optimized.

As discussed in Section 2.4.1, HAZOP seeks to identify hazards by examining the possible failures of components *and the interconnections between components*. A FMEA typically examines only the possible failures of the components. Also, a *team* always performs a HAZOP, while an FMEA may be, and often is, carried out by an *individual*. HAZOP, by using the guide-word-based approach, enables a good team to become very creative as it explores a system's potential hazards. An FMEA, especially if done by a single person using lists of standard fault modes, is far less creative.

As introduced in Section 2.4.2, the starting point of a HAZOP is the search for possible deviations from design intent. When one is found, the study becomes bi-directional: it sets out in one direction (deductively) to find the possible causes of the deviation and in the other (inductively) to evaluate the likely consequences. In this way HAZOP is a creative process in which the team explores the two dimensions of the deviation. On the other hand, an FMEA is uni-directional: on identifying a possible component failure, it proceeds to investigate the likely consequences on the system as a whole. If undesirable consequences are found, a hazard has been identified. This uni-directional approach is less creative, because a HAZOP team exploring the two directions in parallel often perceives interesting interactions that a uni-directional approach misses.

Given that hazards may be caused by deviations from design intent of the components, and interactions between them, and by specific fault modes of the components, it cannot be guaranteed that either HAZOP or FMEA will uncover all hazards and their detailed causes. Indeed, one type of study may disclose the need for the other type.

For example, when a HAZOP throws up a possible deviation from design intent in an interaction between two components, and a possible cause is found to lie in one of the components, the best way of further investigating the detailed cause may be via an FMEA of the component's design. Conversely, when a component is a sub-system with numerous internal sub-components and interactions, and an FMEA has recognised that a possible fault mode is important, a way of investigating further whether the fault mode is plausible may be by a HAZOP. This HAZOP would use a more detailed design representation that displays the interactions between the sub-components of the sub-system.

An FMEA will identify the effects of a fault mode near the component (the local effect) and will then seek to identify how it will affect the system as a whole (the system effect). It is therefore possible to improve the efficiency of the hazard identification by mixing an FMEA of the components with a HAZOP of the interactions between them.

In such a mixed study, only examining the local effects of failures can shorten the FMEA, as studying the interactions between the components during the HAZOP will cover system effects more efficiently. This is based on the fact that local effects cannot have system effects unless they interact with the other components of the system. We term this type of FMEA a 'local effects ' FMEA, and add the caution that it should only be carried out immediately prior to or after using the HAZOP technique to explore the system effects.

It is also worthwhile noting that the fault modes found in an FMEA are often the causes of the deviations found in a HAZOP, and the local effects found in an FMEA are the HAZOP deviations themselves. Thus, HAZOP and FMEA can complement each other, each being a useful guide to the conduct of the other. For example, local effects found during the FMEA may be ignored if they have previously been identified as non-hazardous during a HAZOP. If they have been identified in the HAZOP as hazardous they need not be explored to system level, as the HAZOP will already have done this. This means that, in our experience, the use of HAZOP before an FMEA can result in a more focused and efficient FMEA of the detailed components of a system. And, in general, the complementary use of HAZOP and FMEA on the same design representations produces improved thoroughness and efficiency.

11.5 WHEN TO USE HAZOP AND FMEA

As explained above, HAZOP and inductive techniques such as FMEA are different, but can be complementary. A particular technique can be more effective at given levels of design detail. At others, it may be of less value or even be very difficult or time-consuming to carry out. It is important that the appropriate technique should be selected at a given design stage. It should, however, be noted that it is often the level of design abstraction that determines the selection of the technique, rather than the stage in the life cycle. The decision of whether to use HAZOP or FMEA is often complex, and it requires experience of the particular type of system, the design representations and the different project phases. No absolute rules can be given, but we offer some advice below.

When starting hazard identification and setting out to decide which might be the most appropriate approach to use (whether HAZOP, FMEA or some other technique), a series of questions about the design *at this level of abstraction* should be asked:

1   How much is known about the possible fault modes of the components or sub-systems involved? If little is known, then techniques based on the fault modes of the components, such as FMEA, may be fruitless.

2   Could component or sub-system failure lead directly to hazards, or can hazards also arises through their interactions? If hazards can arise both directly from component or sub-system failure and through their interactions, then both aspects will need to be studied. This suggests that HAZOP on its own will initially be sufficient but that it may then need to be followed by a detailed FMEA of the particular components highlighted by the HAZOP.

3   Can hazards only arise through the interactions of the components?

If this is the case, a study of the interactions using HAZOP may well be sufficient.

4   Are hazards unlikely to be caused by the interactions of the components or sub-systems? If so, a study of interactions may well not be a very useful approach and HAZOP would not be appropriate.

5   If the fault modes of the components are not known, could studying the interactions identify hazards, even if their causes are then unknown? If this is the case, a study of their interactions using HAZOP may produce a useful set of hazards, albeit lacking causes. Once the fault modes are known, further complementary identification using FMEA could be conducted.

6   Have the hazards that might arise due to interactions already been discovered, and is the focus now on the search for their causes and also on the hazards due to component failure? In this case it is probable that the failures of the components will be the causes, so we can study these using FMEA.

Before the study it is almost impossible to answer these questions fully. However, it may well be possible to use an understanding of the particular system, the results of previous studies of it or of similar systems, and the level of design abstraction used to develop a reasonable view on each question. An argument can then be made as to which approach might be best. Once a decision has been made as to which technique should be applied at a particular stage in the life cycle, this should be documented, as should the reasoning behind it. This documentation can then be reviewed as the overall hazard identification and safety analysis process continues and either validated or, even if not validated, used to justify further studies using diverse techniques.

The remainder of this section explains the most likely answers at different levels of design abstraction and thus the approach that might be adopted, although this should be reviewed on a case-by-case basis.

11.5.1   High Levels of Design Abstraction

At high levels of design abstraction, such as in the conceptual design phase, little design information is available, so one is unlikely to be able to answer any of the above questions and would thus be unable to justify a particular technique. There will also be a lack of design information, so systematic techniques may be difficult to apply. As a result, techniques based on historical review, expert review, and 'what if' review are usually more appropriate than a full HAZOP or FMEA.

It is possible that even at such high levels of abstraction the design's interfaces with other systems may be defined. Then, if these interactions might be a cause of hazards, HAZOP is a good tool for studying the interface hazards. However, the more general techniques mentioned above should still be used to review the system for other possible hazards.

When information about the basic components and their general fault modes does become available, a high-level FMEA of all of them may also be carried out. But at this level, in the absence of detailed information on fault modes, a very effective study could be carried out by means of HAZOP. This combination of techniques enables high-level hazards to be identified, and makes subsequent hazard identification easier and more efficient.

11.5.2   Medium Levels of Design Abstraction

As more design detail is developed (for example, for a basic design), the interactions between components become better defined, as do the interactions with other systems. However, the detailed design of components is still likely to be quite poorly defined and the fault modes of the components may not be well understood. At this level the six questions should be carefully reviewed in order to try to identify the best approach.

If interactions are felt to be important, as is often the case, HAZOP is the better technique for checking that the hazard list is complete, that the design copes with hazards already identified, and that mid-level causes of hazards are known.

In cases where interaction hazards are felt to be of little interest, FMEA is more appropriate, but, because one cannot be sure that no interaction hazards exist, we would recommend that some study of interaction hazards be done. It should also be recognised that if the hazards that can arise directly from the failure of single modules, sub-systems or components are not already known, then FMEA should be considered.

At these intermediate levels of design abstraction, studies such as interface hazard identification and analysis (i.e. of the interfaces to other systems) should also be carried out, for which HAZOP is an ideal technique.

So, at intermediate levels of design detail, HAZOP may often be the preferred tool, but it should be supplemented by other techniques.

11.5.3   Low Levels of Design Abstraction

At low levels of design abstraction, such as during the detailed design phase, previous studies should have identified the hazards due to interactions or confirmed that none exist. This means that a fault mode technique such as FMEA is most appropriate.

We have also found that, owing to the large number of interactions that may exist and the difficulties of tracing the deviations from design intent through the complete system, HAZOP is a slow and frustrating exercise which may add little to the hazard identification process. We therefore do not recommend HAZOP at low levels of design abstraction.

As discussed above, if a previous HAZOP has been carried out, it should have identified the undesirable deviations from design intent of the interactions, and these should guide the FMEA and make it more effective, as system effects will normally not need to be examined. The HAZOP will also have indicated which components have the potential to cause system effects through their interactions with the rest of the system. So it may be possible to avoid carrying out an FMEA on the components that cannot have system effects, as determined by the HAZOP.

11.5.4   During Operation

When a study is to be carried out on an operational system, the choice of technique still depends on the level of design abstraction and whether interaction hazards are relevant. Once some initial operational experience is available, and especially if this has shown that interactions are of importance, we recommend a HAZOP of a medium abstraction representation of the system. This could also cover hazard identification for a system which includes the operators (perhaps using the HAZOP-based technique that is described in Chapter 13).

When significant operational experience is available the fault modes of the components can be better confirmed, and it is worthwhile carrying out an FMEA on all the major components, based on the fault modes found during operation. This helps to ensure that failures that occur are formally recorded, particularly if they could have safety implications.

For decommissioning, the choice of approach will again depend on the six questions raised above and the level of design abstraction. It is possible that a study comprising a HAZOP of the interactions involved in the decommissioning process itself, a hazard identification brainstorming session, and a FMEA of the activities involved may be suitable.

11.6 CONCLUDING REMARKS

This chapter has reviewed the reasons why hazard identification needs to be repeated during the life of a system and has identified the times when such studies are required. It has then reviewed and contrasted the HAZOP and FMEA techniques, and given examples of how the decision can be made as to which to apply at particular levels of design abstraction.

12
Dealing with
Particular Difficulties

Three common difficulties can arise in carrying out HAZOP studies. Firstly, when some systems are studied there is an advantage in trying to identify cases where a combination of deviations (i.e. where multiple deviations occur) could lead to a hazard. For example, where the system goes through a repeated cycle of activities, it might be subject to deviations in some attributes simultaneously with deviations in the sequencing or timing of the same or other attributes. HAZOP normally does not consider more than one deviation at a time, and the approach must be modified if multiple deviations are to be considered.

Secondly, the problem of tracking concerns from one representation to another or between the different paper sheets of a single representation often arises, as mentioned in Chapters 4 and 14. To control this process, the study leader must set up a formal system, with rules and a documented procedure.

Thirdly, in many systems, some components and some interconnections between components may not consist of single entities. They may consist of a number of entities that are all present and that form a 'compound' entity or flow. For example, in the chemical industry a pipe between vessels or reactors may carry a mixture of chemicals (a compound flow) some of which may be liquid while others are gaseous. A reactor may contain a mixture of the reacting chemicals, along with the product, these forming a compound entity. In data flow diagrams it is common, especially on representations with a high degree of design abstraction, for what is shown as a single data flow to be in reality a number of different data flows between two components. A data store will often hold more than one type of data, so this may also represent a compound entity. Hazards may arise because of deviations of the individual entities in the compound entity or flow, or because of deviations in the compound entity or flow.

In cases where there is a compound entity or flow, it is essential that the team study each individual entity as well as the compound entity or flow. Doing this requires that the study leader should identify that a compound entity or flow exists on the design representation and correctly plan its study during the HAZOP.

This chapter gives advice on all three of these problems.

12.1 MULTIPLE DEVIATIONS

In a system that goes through a cycle of operation (for example a batch chemical process), or during the start-up or shut-down of a system, aspects of timing, sequence and completeness of actions are often critical to the safety of the system. This means, as discussed in Chapter 4, that the study leader must ensure that the representations used contain all the attributes that could affect safety.

When a full set of representations is available, these should be studied so as to take all of the attributes into account. However, hazards that arise when (and because) multiple deviations occur at the same time can be difficult to identify.

An example of such a problem is a case where a chemical attribute 'flow' may be subject to the deviations 'more' (often abbreviated as flow-more) and 'sequence-early' at the same time. It is possible that a high flow of the material occurring too early in a batch process sequence might cause a different hazard (for example, an extreme excess in pressure if a rapid exothermic reaction were to occur) from either a high flow at the correct time or the correct flow too early in the sequence. The hazards of the combined deviations would be identified only if the team noticed them by chance, as a result of creative exploration during the study. This is because HAZOP normally considers only a single deviation at a time and the identification of hazards due to multiple deviations is not its normal objective. Identification of the hazards from the combined deviation is less likely in the example we have given because the team would normally study the complete representation that contains the attribute 'flow' before studying that which contains the attribute 'sequence'. Thus, there may be a substantial time lag (possibly days or even weeks) between studying the two attributes, reducing the chance of studying the combination of the two deviations and making it less likely that the hazard would be identified.

The problem mentioned above is not infrequent in cyclic systems, where the state of the system changes with time. In systems that operate in a steady state, timing and sequence are not very relevant, so the focus can be on the representation of their steady state. This means that the multiple deviations that could lead to a hazard are likely to be studied at about the same time, which increases the chance of a multiple deviation hazard being noticed. However, in systems where timing and sequence are of importance, multiple representations are required. These will often be studied at different times, increasing the chance that a hazard caused by a multiple deviation is not noticed.

Given that multiple deviations may be of importance in cyclic systems, we recommend that the following approach be used.

Each entity should initially be studied on the main representation for the relevant deviations from design intent of its attributes, assuming that the timing and sequence are correct. The team should then move to the timing and sequencing representations and consider the deviations from design intent for the attributes of the same entity. By doing this on an entity by entity basis, there is a greater chance that hazards caused by multiple deviations are identified.

The above approach cannot guarantee that multiple deviations will be postulated and the hazards resulting from them identified. However, it is our experience that when the representations available for a system make the entity by entity examination possible, it does increase the chance of their coming to light. The approach is possible only if the study leader keeps track of potential combination concerns by running a formal tracking system alongside the HAZOP records discussed in Chapter 10. He or she can then refer back to the HAZOP records generated for the particular entity on the previous representation when the potential combination is studied.

The tracking of these concerns should consist of notes made by the study leader whenever the team foresees a potential multiple deviation. Thus, for example, if the team were to note, when studying flow-more, that this deviation could have serious consequences if the process was not in the correct sequence, the study leader would note, 'It should be studied on the sequence representation,' and ensure that this is done.

12.2 TRACKING OF CONCERNS

A HAZOP will often involve a single representation that is on numerous sheets of paper. In these cases we recommend that only one sheet be studied at a time (until the HAZOP of it is complete), so as to avoid confusion about what is under review. If multiple representations are involved, the team leader should plan how they will be studied (each complete representation in turn or each entity on all representations, as suggested in Section 12.1) and must then ensure that the study follows the plan.

If the approach planned is to study each representation in turn, it is often the case that when studying one representation the team will identify concerns which are not directly related to it and which could be more easily considered on one of the other representations that are scheduled to be studied later. Further, when multiple sheets of paper are needed for one representation, items that are raised on one sheet may sometimes be more easily studied on another. In both these cases there is a temptation for the team either to start to study the other representation or sheet, or, even worse, to attempt to study the deviation on the less than adequate representation or sheet. The study leader needs to be aware of such a tendency and to be prepared to adhere to the planned schedule, otherwise confusion could ensue, with the result that hazards could be missed. The team may well become confused about exactly which sheet or representation they are studying. They may also begin to consider that the other sheets or representations have already been studied, when this is not the case. The result is that when the team later begins to study the other representation or sheet, they may well feel a temptation to take short-cuts. This can lead to a less exhaustive approach and an incomplete study. In order to ensure completeness the study leader should not allow the team to deviate in this way.

A good study leader will control this problem by clearly demonstrating to the team that the concerns which they raise are being recorded, tracked and controlled. Once the team has confidence that this is the case, and that the concerns they raise are not forgotten, they are normally content to study them at a more appropriate point during the HAZOP.

Tracking concerns from sheet to sheet or representation to

representation must be done carefully. When the HAZOP team raises an issue that is better studied on another sheet or representation the study leader must explicitly state his intention to do this. The study leader should then make a formal written record of the need to do so. We recommend that this tracking should not be delegated to another team member, as it is very closely related to the overall control of the HAZOP. Control is the study leader's principal responsibility during the HAZOP meetings.

This formal record is best kept separate from the main HAZOP record (see Figure 12.1 for an example form) and should contain details of the:

- Representation being studied when the point was raised;
- Entity being studied;
- Attribute;
- Guide word;
- Reason for needing to study it on another sheet or representation;
- Sheet or representation the study leader expects to study it on (although this may well change as the study progresses);
- A unique cross-reference that can be used when the concern is finally studied, to enable full cross-referencing. We recommend a numbered note in the HAZOP record.

During the study the study leader should review this formal record when each sheet or representation is finished. This is to verify that all relevant concerns have been addressed, and it serves as a reminder of those which the team need to consider on the next sheet or representation. As concerns are addressed the study leader should note this on the formal record and also on the HAZOP sheet, in the latter case by indicating that an item is related to an earlier item.

Whenever the study leader reviews the formal record used to track such concerns he or she should clearly explain to the team what is being done and the results of the tracking. This helps to build team confidence in the fact that the points are being tracked and addressed, and in the study leader's ability to manage the process. Once the team members have developed such confidence in the study leader, they will no longer wish to study every concern when it is first identified.

At the end of the HAZOP the leader must ensure that all the points which require inter-sheet or representation tracking have been closed-out and should review the formal record with the HAZOP team. If concerns have not been closed-out, then the team should re-examine them and ensure closure. We would normally include the leader's tracking system as part of the HAZOP record.

Company XXX

HAZOP Records

HAZOP inter-representation tracking sheet

Repr.	Sheet	Entity	Attribute	Guide word	Reason and where it is most likely to be studied	Description	Closed?

Figure 12.1: Typical form used to track concerns between sheets or representations

12.3 COMPOUND FLOWS AND ENTITIES

Compound entities and flows, as introduced in Section 4.1.5, are common in the chemical industry (mixtures of chemicals often flow in the same pipe or exist in the same reactor) and in programmable systems. Ultimately, it is the primitive single-item flows that need to be studied at some time during one of the HAZOP studies conducted. If only one HAZOP is carried out, on a single level of design (typical for chemical plant P&ID diagrams), the individual flows must be identified and addressed at that level. In other cases, when a hierarchical decomposition is available (as for many programmable systems), it is usual to look at the primitive flows when the decomposition reaches the appropriate level. We shall look at these two situations in turn.

First, compound flows of chemicals. As the chemical mixture is a group, it is common practice to consider the attributes of the group as well as to add other attributes specifically for compound flows, for example the attributes 'composition' and 'state' (how these attributes would be used and how the resultant interpretations would be identified are addressed in Section 7.2 of Chapter 7). However, it is possible that one chemical could be subject to different deviations from the other ones present, and if this is not studied a hazard could be missed. For example, if two chemicals have been poorly mixed they may form layers and their temperatures could deviate in different ways.

When considering such a compound flow or entity the approach we recommend is to consider each part of it as a separate entity. For example, in a chemical process this would mean studying each chemical present in the flow. Each entity should be taken in turn and subjected to the systematic examination of its attributes, guide words and interpretations. It should be noted that some of the attributes might be identical for all the entities — for example all the chemicals will normally be at the same pressure in a pipe.

Once all the entities have been studied the team should apply the attributes and guide words to the flow as a whole to investigate the effects that possible deviations of the complete flow might have. Finally, they should apply any special guide words that have been developed for compound flows such as 'composition', 'part of' and 'state'.

This approach has the advantage of being highly systematic. It can be used to show that an exhaustive study has been done and that allowance has been made for those cases where the different entities could deviate from design intent in different ways.

The HAZOP record should clearly indicate each entity as it is studied in turn and then record the final application of the attribute-guide-word combinations to the overall flow. Although this approach may initially seem laborious, the majority of attributes are often found to be common to all the entities involved and so can be studied together.

This approach raises the question of how a team should study the cases where two compounds could have two different deviations at the same time (for example one could have flow-less while another has temperature-more). In essence this is the same as any other case that could occur in any system where two attributes deviate from design intent at the same time and is addressed above in Section 12.1.

Second, compound flows are also common in PES representations, as introduced in Section 7.4. In data flow diagrams the flow on an interconnection may be anything from a single data item to a group of any number of items. Again, it is necessary to study the attributes of each item. On a high-level diagram, a single interconnection may be descriptive of the whole group. Decomposition into subgroups and then into primitive single-item flows takes place on successively more detailed design representations. It is usual to look at the primitive flows when the decomposition reaches the appropriate level.

Sometimes, the team doing a study that includes high-level compound flows will discover a need to consider the primitive flows, in order to explore deviations of the compound flows. In this case the HAZOP leader should allow the team to study the primitive flows but a cautionary note is necessary. It can be tempting, when the team is aware that further design detail is available, to begin exploring deviations at a lower level than is appropriate at the time. This can lead to an unstructured study and inconsistent results, so the HAZOP leader must keep the focus at the intended level.

Another potential problem is when a compound interconnection bifurcates between components, so that one part of the flow goes to one receiving component and the remainder to another receiving component — or when a data signal is transmitted to two different recipients. When this occurs, the matter is simplified if they are addressed as two separate interconnections between the sending component and the two receiving components. Similarly, a bi-directional interconnection between components should be addressed as separate interconnections in the two directions.

12.4 CONCLUDING REMARKS

This chapter has discussed three difficulties that can arise during HAZOPs and has recommended how they should be managed. It has explained:

- How to improve the chance of detecting hazards due to the effects of combined deviations from design intent;
- How to track concerns that might be noted on one representation or sheet of a representation, but which are better studied on another;
- How to control the HAZOP process when a single item on a representation may represent more than one entity.

13
HAZOP of Human-centred Systems

This chapter describes an approach to the identification of hazards in human-centred systems, in which the human component is central or critical to system functionality or safety. The approach was developed by Cambridge Consultants Limited and Arthur D. Little, and has been given the name 'SUSI', an acronym for Safety analysis of User System Interaction.

In recent years there has been an increasing realization that consideration of the place of the human in a system (human factors) should be an integral part of system design. Indeed, a failure of the human operator is often cited as the cause of system failure. Human failures may occur in two different ways:

- As an 'error' where the operator intends to work correctly, but fails to do so (e.g. gets two steps in a procedure muddled up);
- As a 'violation' (see [Mason 97]) where the operator acts contrary to requirements because (for example):
    - there is no precedent for the situation and the 'correct' action is not defined;
    - a shortcut saves time;

— it has 'always been done this way'.

Usually, what has happened is that the operator has behaved in a way other than that intended or expected by the designer. In part, that behaviour can be explained by operators not having a full understanding of their expected role in the system. However, in many situations it is because of a shortcoming in the overall design of the user interaction — particularly in respect of the occurrence of an unexpected event. In these circumstances, it is hardly fair to blame the operator for what is a failure of the overall system design. The fact remains, however, that once an incident occurs, we normally identify human error as the root cause [Westrum 91].

When we consider the design and implementation of computer-based systems involving significant human interaction, we find that at least three specialists should be involved:

- Those who design functionality;
- Those who design the details of the user interface;
- Those human factors specialists who examine how particular tasks are carried out.

In order to build effective, safe systems, it is clear that all three specialists must be involved and must communicate with each other. However, the reality is that the three areas all have their own specialist vocabularies and models of the system, and they tend to work independently of each other. In addition, industries which have an established record of building safety-critical systems are likely to have specialists in safety. These personnel, too, have their own particular vocabulary and often may not be familiar with the techniques of developing computer-based systems. This lack of coordination between the specialists during system development has the potential to lead to hazardous situations. Further, in many safety analysis methods the identification of hazards is carried out separately for the human tasks and the machine functionality. Where the interactions between the human tasks and the machine processes are complex, hazards may be missed if the full scope of the interactions is not studied.

The SUSI approach systematically identifies hazards of human or machine origin for human-centred systems. SUSI comprises two parts:

- A common representation of all entities in systems, so that communication between specialists is enabled;
- A structured, hazard identification procedure (HAZOP) which also addresses features that are particular to human-machine interactions.

This chapter concentrates on the representation aspects because the hazard identification uses exactly the same process as that described in earlier chapters. An explanation of representation in Section 13.1 is followed in Section 13.2 by a discussion of HAZOP guide-word interpretations for human-centred systems. To illustrate the practical application of the approach, an example is given in Section 13.3 of a medical laboratory imaging system.

13.1 REPRESENTING HUMAN-MACHINE SYSTEMS

Hazard identification requires an appropriate description of the system which can be inspected. Where the interaction between human tasks and machine processes is concerned, there is a need for a common representation. Below we offer a description of human-centred task analysis and guidance on building the representation of the system that can be used for the later hazard identification. This description is given in more detail than that in Chapter 7 on other design representations because it is likely to be new to many readers and there is little other guidance available.

We have found that a large range of human-centred systems are based on information transfer and processing, particularly if information transfer is taken to include paper and object movements together with voice communications. By considering the overall system as one of information transfer, it is possible to use conventional information flow representations in order to develop a total system description.

13.1.1   Describing Human-based Systems

The method used to represent human-based systems has been borrowed from the domain of software engineering. The growth of structured design methods in software development has led to a variety of conventions for producing an explicit representation of a system. Key among these are various data flow, control flow, process flow and state transition representations, known collectively as structured design. These various descriptions provide a powerful means of representing the software design and are more or less suitable for differing categories of software systems. The conventions of structured design, together with the extensions proposed by Hatley and Pirbhai [Hatley 88], provide a good framework for describing (in models) both the data and the processes within a system and the control flow information. The conventional use of the Hatley-Pirbhai method is for software-based, typically real-time, systems. In our work we have found that the basic representation techniques are general in application. In particular, in the context of this chapter, we are concerned with system representations that combine human and machine activity. Therefore, the modelling method needs to show the human tasks as well as the machine processes within the same representation.

The basis of the approach is to adopt a consistent notation for representing the human tasks and machine processes, and the data and control flows between the tasks and the processes. Such an approach is valid as long as the human activity is information-intensive, such as:

- Taking decisions based on information received;
- Transferring information between parts of a system;
- Classifying and sorting the information in a system.

The notation is less representative when the human tasks depend on significant motor skills or introspective reasoning components. An example of a situation where motor skills take a prominent part is the interaction between the driver of a Formula 1 racing car and the active computer systems used to manage many of the car's mechanical functions. Here, there is intuitive feedback between man and machine that is far more subtle than just the straightforward processing of information. If there is a need to model such interactions, then one of the standard texts such as Sanders and McCormick [Sanders 93] should be consulted.

However, much human work falls into the information-intensive class, especially where automation is used to remove the manual labour aspects of jobs, and here a data flow and process model for the human components of a system can help generate an integrated representation of the overall system. Using this we can explore the identification of hazards in a consistent manner across the whole system.

Figure 13.1 illustrates the conventions used in this type of representation. The representation follows the notation of Hatley and Pirbhai, except that data flows and control flows are shown on the same representation. The key components are:

- A circle represents a machine process or human task;
- A solid line is a data or information flow and can include speech;
- A dashed line is a control flow (stop, start, alarm, etc.) and can include spoken commands;
- Two parallel lines represent a data store. One addition we make to the convention is to show screen displays as data stores (with the justification that the data may be written to a screen, but there has to be an explicit human process to read the data).

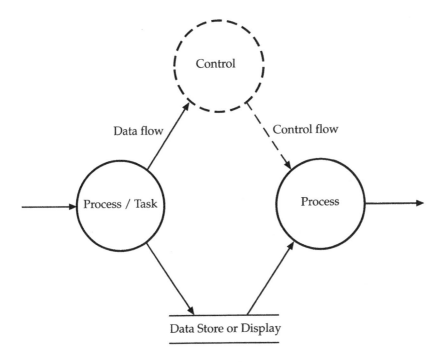

Figure 13.1: Process and data flow representation

13.1.2　Developing the System Model

In order to develop a representation of the system model it is necessary to consider the human tasks and the machine processes working together as a total system. For existing systems there may already be a description of the functions associated with the machine processes, and in some cases there will be task descriptions of the human activities. Both of these can be used as source documents in building the integrated description of an existing system. The principal steps in developing an integrated description are:

- Identifying the goals of the system (what its purposes are);
- Defining the constraints (which might limit the possible solutions);
- Defining the boundary between the system and the rest of the world;
- Decomposing the basic functions that need to be carried out until human tasks and machine processes can be separately identified.

The above steps are necessary when considering the design of a new human-centred system, but they have also been found useful when examining an existing system where the human has not been included in any design representation that might already exist. Each of the steps will now be examined in more detail, assuming a new system is to be designed.

(a)   Identifying the Goals

All systems should have defined goals (or purposes). The functions necessary to the system will be those that satisfy the goals. Some goals can be generated by identifying those people who have an interest in the system and translating their particular viewpoints into goals for the system. The process of finding out the views of interested or involved parties is known as 'stakeholder analysis'. As an example of this we can take the case of a computer-assisted medical sample inspection process where the principal functional goal of the system is the identification of abnormalities in the samples. Reviewing the objectives of the various interested parties throws up additional goals from their points of view:

- Patients: a reliable system which does not produce false reports;
- Doctors: provision of reports which can be interpreted easily for diagnosis;
- Health Service: an efficient system that also includes quality control;
- Management: a system which produces auditable data;
- Staff: feedback on individual performance.

(b)   Defining the Constraints

In designing any new system, there are likely to be factors which limit (constrain) the possible design solutions. These factors can usefully be thought of as being in two categories: those imposed by outside issues of policy, and those imposed as a result of what is possible with existing technology. Policy issues include:

- Legal and regulatory aspects;
- Standards such as safe working practices;
- Decisions made by the owner about such things as:
    - interworking with other systems;
    - responsibility and authority structures (e.g. whether the operator retains overall control);
    - procurement strategy.

Technology constraints include issues such as:

- The maturity of the technology;
- The expected lifetime of the system;
- The size and speed (response speed or speed of repeatability) of the proposed system.

The constraints impose limits on the functionality that can be achieved by the system and are likely to have a significant impact on the way functions are partitioned between human tasks and machine processes.

(c)   Defining the Boundary

A boundary is defined where there is an entity with which the system must exchange data but which is outside the controlled authority of the system under study. The goals and constraints define the principal boundaries between the system and the external world. It is crucial to remember that a variety of human roles will exist within the system. In many cases a simple guideline when setting boundaries is that it is best to partition so that the majority of an individual's job is either inside or outside the boundary. Again, in line with the fundamental principles of structured design, boundaries should be as simple as possible with a minimum of data exchanges across them. Thus if we take the case of the computer-assisted medical inspection system, the doctors and clinics which supply patient samples and laboratory management can conveniently be placed outside the system boundary, while the medical staff and technicians who carry out the sample investigations are placed within it.

A further test of the boundary condition is to consider the circumstance where the functions are performed by humans only, and then to ask the question, 'Where is the organisation's boundary for the division of tasks between the different sets of humans involved?' Envisaging a fully manual implementation of the medical inspection system naturally leads to the same boundary as that given above.

(d)   Decomposing the Functions

Once goals, constraints and boundaries are defined, functions can be decomposed. It is likely that as functions are defined in more detail, knowledge of the data exchanges across the boundaries will be refined. It may be that consideration at lower levels shows up the need for an interface to an external entity that has not been defined at the top level. Such additional interfaces should be rare if the analysis has been carried out correctly.

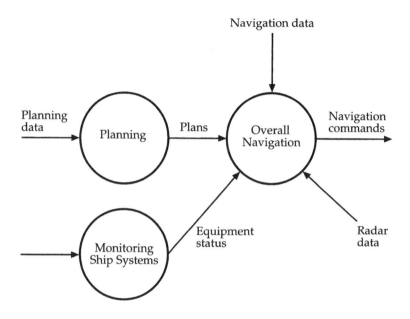

Figure 13.2: Top-level decomposition of ship navigation

The objective of the functional decomposition is to get to, at least, the level where human tasks can be separated from machine processes. The modelling approach uses exactly the same symbols for machine and human tasks and communication between tasks. This is a great advantage when designing new systems, as the generic solution to a problem can be modelled at an abstract level and the decisions on the division of responsibilities then made to give the most efficient implementation. Care must be taken to avoid separation at too high a level. A decomposition will not be effective if its first level places humans separate from machines. At the first level there *may* be machine-only or human-only functions, but these should be rare.

Later in this chapter, a totally different application is chosen to show that the principles may be applied in a variety of areas. Here, ship navigation is used as an example (see Figure 13.2). At the top level we have a decomposition into overall navigation, planning and monitoring systems. At this level planning is separated since much of it takes place before a voyage commences and is therefore characterised by needing information much earlier. 'Monitoring ship systems' is shown as a separate process since the purpose is to collect data from disparate systems and pass on to the overall navigation function a simple statement of equipment status and capability.

At the next level we can decompose the overall navigation functions into principal functions:

- Navigation — the avoidance of fixed objects;
- Collision avoidance — the avoidance of moving objects.

Since the output of these two may produce conflicting solutions a third function of decision taking is required (often referred to as 'conning') — see Figure 13.3.

At this level of decomposition we can identify that the decision taking function (conning) is principally human. Navigation and collision avoidance, on the other hand, include the use of significant machine processes such as geographical positioning systems and radar systems as well as human activities.

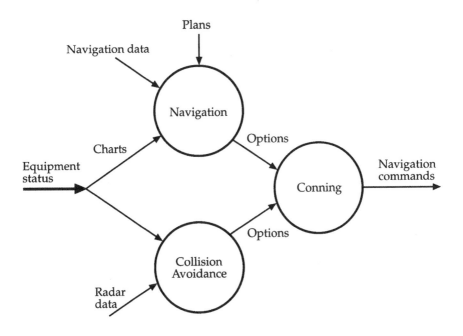

Figure 13.3: Decomposition of overall navigation

i) Models of decision making

In many cases the initial stages of decomposition are fairly straightforward. However, in those cases where it is not clear what the functional decomposition is, generic models of decision making may need to be consulted. We have found through work in a number of areas that where the decision making process is principally concerned with control or management of data, gathering and action execution functions, a model as shown in Figure 13.4 can be used. Its elements are as follows:

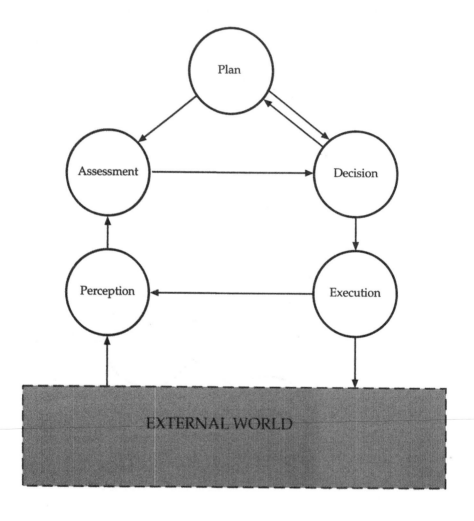

Figure 13.4: Generic control model

- Perception — interpretation of input signals and their amalgamation into a form which facilitates reasoning about them, often referred to as data fusion;
- Assessment — interpretation of the fused input data to develop an understanding of the situation, usually done in the context of how the external world is expected to behave;
- Plan — development of expectations about how the situation is likely to develop and definition of actions to meet those expectations,
- Decision — selection of action options in the context of plans and situation assessment;
- Execution — carrying out of the actions.

An example of this model is an operator controlling a railway signal box. There is information about the state of signals, the settings of the points, and the positions of the trains (external world). This information is taken in and interpreted by the signalman (perception) to build up a picture about the current state of the railway (assessment). The signalman will have details of the expected timetable (plan) and will use that information together with the assessment of the current state of the railway to come to decisions about the future settings of the signals and points to provide the best flow of trains. This might involve changes to the published timetable and so result in a revised plan. Execution is the sending of commands to the external world to change signals and points in order to implement the decisions.

Alternative models of decision making have been developed in the field of artificial intelligence. A comprehensive source of such models can be found in [Schreiber 93].

ii) The decomposition process

The basis of the decomposition is to take a top-down approach to understanding system functions and their relationships. As the process of functional decomposition proceeds, the information flows at each level must be consistent with those at the level above.

The decomposition should follow the guidance given for structured design in, for instance, [Hatley 88]. It is a general rule that at each level of decomposition there should be no more than around seven processes or tasks. However, there is a trade-off between simplicity at any level (i.e. fewer processes or tasks) and the depth of the hierarchy. If the decomposition is deep with few processes or tasks at each level, there will need to be continuous referrals up and down the hierarchy to understand the interactions.

Although not shown in the examples given, the approach can model human-to-human interactions in the same way as human-computer interactions. For human-to-human interactions, entities such as human memory and knowledge can be represented as (imperfect!) data stores.

Where a very large number of processes or tasks are defined at a particular level, consideration should be given to grouping some of them together and representing their decomposition at a lower level. If this is done, the grouping should be chosen to comply with the general principle of minimising the number of data flows between the group and all other processes or tasks.

13.1.3 Using Other Representations

The majority of the above discussion is function-centred, and tasks are examined as far as they contribute to carrying out the function. Thus, when an operator carries out a group of tasks that form a coherent 'job element', and that contributes to a particular function, then the approach described normally works well.

However, humans often have to complete in a particular timescale several tasks which contribute to different functions (e.g. starting up a complex system). Here, modelling the individual functions may give no indication of the total workload or the pressures the human may be under, so hazards might be missed. A full system description will often need to include representations which consider the timing of different tasks and the dynamic interactions between them.

In addition, where control processes are identified, it may be necessary to analyse them in terms of a state transition representation, especially where there are complex relationships between the states.

13.2 HAZOP FOR HUMAN-CENTRED SYSTEMS

An effective way to identify hazards in human-centred systems which have been modelled using the principles introduced in Section 13.1 above, is by a HAZOP, looking at deviations from design intent of the processes and tasks and the information flowing between them.

Because the study will be exploring deviations from design intent by the human as well as the machine parts of the system, we recommend that at least one member of the team should have a good knowledge of human factors. This will help ensure that the full scope and nature of human error is considered [Reason 90].

Sometimes, when an analysis of a system is needed, only a partial model of it will exist (usually one without the human tasks), or there may be separate models for the automated and human activities. Our experience is that generating an integrated model is necessary to enable effective hazard identification, taking any partial models as source documents. As techniques mature, we expect that models such as we describe will be produced routinely during system design. As the human and machine parts will have different fault modes, it is important that the representation be annotated with information about which processes are machine only, which are human only, and which are a combination of the two. This implies that the representation must be at such a level that the optimum division between human and machine is clear, as described in Section 13.1.2 *(d)*.

13.2.1   Guide Word Interpretations for Human-centred Systems

For the case of human tasks, a specific set of interpretations for the guide words given in Chapter 7 has been produced, as shown in Table 13.1. Some

Table 13.1: Guide word interpretations for human tasks

Attribute	Guide word	Interpretation
Process/Task	No	Does not happen
	As well as	Additional tasks undertaken or part repeated
	Part of	Only part of task executed
	Other than	Wrong task executed
Human control process	No	Control action does not take place
	As well as	Additional unwanted action takes place
	Part of	Action incomplete
	Other than	Action incorrect
Sequencing	Before/after	Action out of expected order
	Early	Action takes place before an expected time
	Late	Action takes place after an expected time
	No	No action

Table 13.2: Guide word interpretations for data flow (including human-to-human)

Attribute	Guide word	Interpretation
Flow (of data or control)	No	No information flow
	As well as	There is some additional information
	Part of	Information passed is incomplete
	Other than	Information complete but incorrect
	More	More data is passed than expected
Speech data flow between humans	No	They do not (or cannot) communicate
	As well as	Recipient hears originator but someone else talking causes confusion
	Part of	Recipient only hears part of message (possibly because of noise)
	Other than	The originator gives the wrong information or it is totally misunderstood
	More	The originator says more than is necessary
Data to/from data store	No	Data not stored or not found
	As well as	Data store contains more items than expected
	Part of	Data store is incomplete
	Other than	Data changed in store
Data to/from human memory	No	Human either did not register the information or has forgotten it
	As well as	The human gives more information than is asked for
	Part of	Memory is fallible and some of the information is forgotten
	Other than	Memory is fallible and completely wrong information is given

of the data flow interpretations for flow between both machines and humans are shown in Table 13.2.

Note the differences in interpretations that are necessary when flows to or from humans are considered. For example, as mentioned in Section 13.1.1, a data store can be a display screen, in which case an explicit human action is needed to read it. Similarly, human memory may also be considered as a data store, and of course in this case, given the fallibility of human memory, many of the interpretations will be relevant!

Data flow can, of course, mean data transfer by speech. As an example, consider speech between two people in a noisy environment. Here, the originator may state the information correctly, but it may not all be heard by the recipient and the guide word 'part of' would have a valid interpretation. Similarly, if the recipient is able to hear the originator correctly but is being talked to by a third party at the same time, then the guide word 'as well as' will have a valid interpretation.

13.3 EXAMPLE HAZOP OF A MEDICAL DIAGNOSTIC SYSTEM

13.3.1 Medical Imaging System

The example system is an experimental version of a semi-automated system for the screening of cervical smear samples to identify abnormalities which might lead to cancer. It was produced by the Human Genetics Unit (HGU) of the Medical Research Council in Edinburgh, working with the Department of Pathology of the University of Edinburgh. A full description of the work of which this hazard identification is part may be found in [CCL 95]. It was carried out as a collaboration between three organisations, the Centre for Software Engineering, Cambridge Consultants, and the HGU.

Within a cytology laboratory, the semi-automated equipment will consist of two major parts, a robot slide preparation system (RSPS) and a slide scanning system (SSS). The RSPS takes in sample bottles submitted by GPs or clinics and transfers a part of the material as a monolayer sample on to slides.

The SSS is an image processing system which inspects objects on the slide and classifies them. When abnormal objects are identified, the system stores digitised images for subsequent human inspection. Both the above systems are supported by a computer-based system providing overall administration and interfacing to the laboratory main computer where patient records are stored.

13.3.2 Development of the Data Flow Description

The full system description is complex and an overview is given in [CCL 95]. Here, we offer simplified versions of the top three levels of the description to illustrate the method (the full description has six levels in the hierarchical decomposition). The system context (the highest level 0) identifies the complete system under consideration and its principal interactions with the external world. Here there are three external entities:

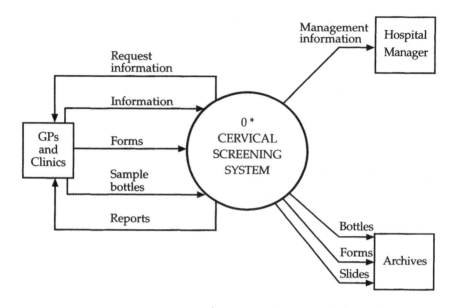

Figure 13.5: Context diagram for medical imaging system

the clinics or surgeries which collect samples and to which reports are returned, the hospital management systems and, within the laboratory, the archives where reports and samples are stored. Note that the total screening system includes the human administrators, technicians and medical personnel who interact with the machine sub-systems. Figure 13.5 gives the context diagram. Note the convention that '*' by the number of a process shows that there is a lower-level expansion of that process.

The top-level system is then decomposed whilst preserving the external data flows. Figure 13.6 shows level 1, the division into four processes:

- Sample and form validation — this receives specimens and forms, checks the consistency of data, and enters the data into the laboratory administration computer;
- Preparation and scanning — this includes the preparation of the slides and the scanning by the automated slide-scanning system;
- Review process — this covers the manual review of slides, using on-screen images and microscope examination;
- Laboratory administration computer — this stores the results of the processing.

For the next level of decomposition, we show the expansion of only one

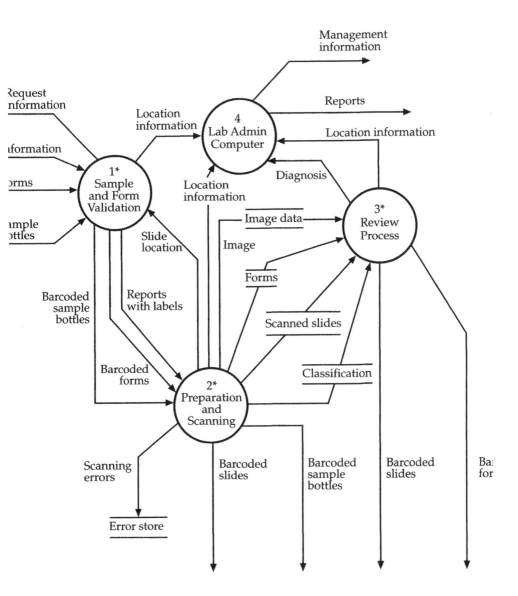

Figure 13.6: Top-level breakdown of medical laboratory system

process, and Figure 13.7 gives that decomposition for the first (semi-manual) part of the preparation and scanning process. Note in the figure that process 1 is the sample and form validation process shown in Figure 13.6, process 4 is that of the laboratory administration computer and, in

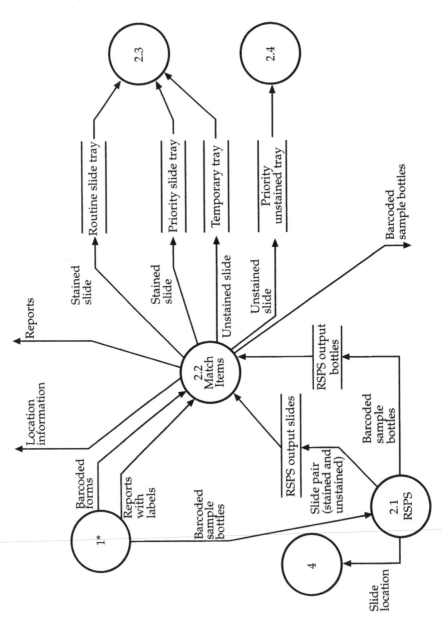

Figure 13.7: Part of the decomposition of the preparation and scanning process

order not to complicate the figure, the flows out of processes 2.3 and 2.4 are not shown.

Process 2.1 (Robot slide preparation system — RSPS) takes the specimen bottles and produces two slides from each specimen. In modelling the system it was necessary to include an explicit process, shown in Figure 13.7 as '2.2 Match Items', because the automated part of the system had few opportunities to cross-check for errors in the pairing of patient forms and patient sample bottles. It is a key and intensive human process which achieves the following: cross-checking, visual quality assessment of prepared slides, attachment of a label to each slide, and assignment of samples for priority processing where there are clinical indications. To aid the human to carry out the process, a screen is used to display status information and a barcode reader pen is used to cross-check barcoded items against patient details.

The data flow design was produced by a team of a consultant, a cytopathologist and a member of the design team of the experimental automated system. The team approach ensured that the various viewpoints on the design were captured in an effective manner and activities were partitioned between human and machine in a way that was readily understandable to all those involved. This level of common understanding had not been achieved previously, despite regular and detailed liaison.

13.3.3   Application of HAZOP

The HAZOP team was as we recommend in Chapter 6. The study leader role was taken by someone who was an experienced study leader but had no direct involvement in other parts of the work. Representatives of both the design team and the intended users of the system were present, together with an expert in human factors so that human error could be explored effectively.

The objective of the hazard identification was to examine the preliminary design of the automated screening system to identify hazardous situations which would need to be addressed in subsequent design stages. The HAZOP process thus focused on two types of issue. One of these related to design aspects which would enhance operability and safety, and the other was to identify practical constraints which would impact on the viability or safety of the system. For the latter category, the practical knowledge of cytotechnologists and laboratory technicians (the 'users' in the HAZOP team) was invaluable.

Table 13.3 gives part of the HAZOP recording sheet for the 'match items'

Table 13.3: Sample HAZOP sheet for match items process

HAZOP item	Item	Attribute	Guide word	Cause	Consequence / implication	Indication /protection	Question/ recommendation
1	Barcoded form	Data flow	Other than	Mismatch of names when checked against sample	Wrong patient matched to slide	Name on form and bottle	Manual double-check
2	Match items process	Task	Other than	Failure to select correct report /label combination	Wrong patient matched to slide	Name on form and bottle	Print report and label on same form and have the label as tear-off
3	Match items process	Task	Part of	Report available but no label	Delay in process	Slide and report but no label	Print report and label on same form and have the label as tear-off
4	Slide pair	Data flow	Other than	Mislocation of slides	Wrong patient matched to slide	Accession number and barcode mismatch	Scan barcodes as check
5	Slide pair	Data flow	No	Report precedes slide to RSPS	Delay in process	Report but no slide	Only print report once slide produced

process, with recording of only those items where hazards were identified. From the HAZOP sheet we see that some of the principal recommendations recorded during analysis of the 'match items' process were:

- Cross-checking the original matching of patient form and sample to avoid the wrong patient being matched to the slide (this can be a problem with patients called, for instance, M Smith, Margaret Smith and Maggie Smith);
- Printing the patient report and the label to be attached to the slide on the same form and having the label as tear-off to avoid a mismatch or a delay in the process, by ensuring that the report and the label do not get separated until the label is to be stuck on the slide;
- Scanning barcodes as a check that the slides in the slide tray are in the correct order so that the wrong patient does not get matched to the slide (each patient will be matched to the correct slide by a unique barcode).

An interesting design decision which came out of the recommendation to have tear-off labels was that two people are needed to carry out the 'match items' process: one (wearing surgical gloves) to handle the sample bottles and the other to stick the label on the slide because it is almost impossible to handle sticky labels when wearing gloves.

13.4 CONCLUDING REMARKS

In this chapter we have described a methodology for the identification of hazards in human-centred systems. The key points are:

- Data flow analysis is an effective tool for modelling both human and machine tasks and to produce an integrated representation of the total system;
- A process for developing this model has been described;
- We find that designers with different viewpoints are able to use the common representation and that its use increases their understanding of the total system;
- Operators and users find the representation easy to understand, to comment on and to check at a detailed level — something they often are not able to do with a variety of specialist models;
- Hazard identification can then effectively be carried out on the resulting model using HAZOP, studying deviations of the human and machine processes as well as the data flowing between them.

14
HAZOP of Systems in an Environment that Changes during Operation

Our experience reveals that a system having to operate in a changing environment presents problems to the HAZOP process. In this context, the environment is the world within which the system is set and with which it interacts. The changes can occur over long periods of time, but more often they do so as the system goes through a cycle of operation.

This is a problem to which no established solution exists. This chapter explains an approach we have used and found useful, and it thus gives guidance on how such systems can be studied during a HAZOP.

We include in the environment of a system such aspects as the human-machine interface and its respective operating instructions, interfaces with other systems, and external influences such as electromagnetic interference.

One example, on which we have done a substantial number of

HAZOPs, is the computer-based railway signalling system that is used to stop trains from going too fast, and to prevent them from passing red signals or approaching dangerous situations. Typically, such systems are called automatic train protection (ATP). The environment of the ATP system changes as the train travels, as described below.

The ATP system on board the train interfaces with a small number of mechanical and human systems, such as the brakes, doors, train driver and passengers. While the train travels down the line the main changes with respect to these other systems are in the opening and closing of the doors — which the ATP will often either control or monitor in order to check that they open only in stations and on the platform side. However there is also a trackside ATP system. The on-board system interfaces with it as well, and it in turn interfaces with numerous other railway systems, for example, points, ventilation systems, and passenger emergency plungers on platforms (which are used to attempt to stop the trains if someone falls on to the track).

The trackside ATP sends the on-board ATP information about the status of the other trackside systems, as well as any changes to the speed limits on the line and the positions of the trains ahead. The trackside ATP equipment is relatively complex. It can include components on or near the track that interface directly with the on-board ATP to help determine certain items. For example, the on-board ATP may require information to enable it to do such diverse functions as re-calibrate the train's location, check the wheel diameter for wear during operation (as this affects speed and distance measurement), and even decide whether the on-board system should or should not be active.

In a typical 'train-day', the train leaves the depot at the start of service. If the depot is not ATP equipped, it enters ATP mode. At the end of service, it exits from ATP mode and enters the depot. As the train travels down the track in ATP mode, the environment of the on-board ATP system will change during the course of the journey. Examples of the environments it passes through include:

- When the train is stationary at a station, but the doors are closed;
- When the train is stationary at a station and the doors are open with passengers exiting and entering the train;
- As the doors are closing at the station;
- As the train accelerates and leaves the station;
- When the train travels down the track it will pass all the different types of trackside systems and, as these change, the on-board ATP

> encounters a myriad of different environments, which change from
> instant to instant;
- When it encounters potential emergencies, each of which presents a
  particular environment;
- When it brakes and halts at the next station, and the process is
  repeated.

Another aspect that needs to be considered is that the ATP might have two
or more modes of operation. For example, in 'automatic' mode the on-
board ATP will monitor the speed of the train to ensure that it does not
exceed the safe speed limit, and it will also monitor the distance to any
stopping point ahead of the train so as to ensure that the train does not
enter a hazardous situation by, for example, approaching too close to
another train or to a set of points in an incorrect position. In 'restricted'
mode the ATP will simply limit the train speed to a low value, such as 20
kph, and will not monitor the distance to other trains or obstacles. In
'restricted' mode the driver is responsible for ensuring that the train does
not physically enter a hazardous situation. From time to time the situation
will arise when the on-board ATP is required to protect the train when
either the on-board or trackside ATP system has more limited functionality
or even when one of the systems has failed.

As the train passes each trackside system (for example points,
ventilation systems, and passenger emergency plungers on platforms, as
mentioned above) to which the trackside ATP interfaces, the trackside ATP
will generate information that either causes the train to stop or to continue.
The hazards involved will depend on the on-board ATP mode, the position
and speed of the train, and on the behaviour of the other trains around it.
By definition, the trains around it include those ahead, those behind, and
those which have routes that converge with or cross its own.

The hazards may also change in nature and criticality, based on the
number of passengers on board the train and the status of the other
trackside systems present in a particular section of track. However, while
all these changes of environment occur, the basic functionality of the system
remains the same and its internal architecture does not change.

But while using this ATP example in the following discussion, let us
not forget that it is only an example, a vehicle to illustrate the application
of the HAZOP approach described in this chapter.

14.1 SPECIAL PROBLEMS FOR THIS TYPE OF HAZOP

When doing a HAZOP of a system which changes its environment as time passes, the main problem is how to achieve cost-effectiveness while still ensuring completeness.

If a system can be in a number of discrete environments, then it is possible to carry out a HAZOP by studying each environment in a particular series of HAZOP meetings.

This approach would require that representations of the system in each environment are made available, entities and attributes identified, and guide words and interpretations defined. The HAZOP would also need to consider the timing diagrams and state transition diagrams (or other suitable representations) that describe how the system changes between environments. It would also require that the study be planned to allow for this kind of approach to be taken.

We have found that there are a number of problems with this type of approach:

- Firstly, it is very time-consuming to do this, especially if a large number of environments need to be examined.
- Secondly, a large amount of repetition is involved, because the deviations from design intent are very similar in many of the environments.
- Thirdly, we have found that the above two factors reduce the concentration of the HAZOP team and thus lead to a loss of effectiveness and efficiency.
- Fourthly, concerns may be raised while studying one environment that are better studied in another. The need to track concerns typically arises either when the team identifies that a deviation from design intent in one environment will need to be re-examined in another, or when the team identifies a potential concern that needs to be considered in an environment that is still to be studied. The team will then need to remember this, so a tracking system is required. In these cases the study leader should note the concerns and then raise them at the correct time. However, the tracking and controlling of concerns between environments is not easy and will need to be managed carefully. Tracking problems are more likely to occur if the study leader is not skilled in this area, and Section 12.2 gives guidance on the tracking of concerns.
- Finally, in some cases the number of potential environments will simply be too large to allow an environment-by-environment

approach. If we take the case of the on-board ATP system, we can, from the description given above, identify a large number of environments during the train-day. Our experience has shown that in this complex case it is not realistic to apply the environment-by-environment approach.

14.2 STUDYING MULTIPLE ENVIRONMENTS

These problems led us to investigate alternative approaches. After several trials we developed the approach described below, that is efficient whilst still remaining exhaustive.

The team first needs to define all the interactions that the system has with its changing environment, which should be noted on the representations to be used during the HAZOP. In the case of the ATP system, the changing interactions would include the interfaces between the trackside ATP and most of the other systems on the railway, as changes in the other systems affect the environment of the ATP.

For example, if the railway has tunnels that pass under rivers, and these are fitted with flood gates at both ends, the flood gate interfaces would be identified. This is because in each of the different train environments with respect to the flood gates, there may be different hazards. The environments include:

*   When the train is sufficiently far away to stop before the flood gate;
*   When the train is too close and cannot stop in time;
*   When the train is immediately beneath the gate;
*   When the train is in the tunnel between the flood gates.

The hazards would include:

*   The gate comes down, but failure of the train braking system means that the train does not stop;
*   The gate comes down and the train collides with it;
*   The gate comes down on top of the train;
*   Both gates come down and the train is trapped in a flooded tunnel.

Having defined all the interactions between the system and the changing environment and noted them on the representation, the team is able to understand clearly the boundaries of the system within its environments (as the boundaries are defined by the interactions). All the interactions defined in this manner will need to be examined during the HAZOP.

As far as this approach is concerned, aspects of the system's environment that do not change may be considered during the HAZOP meeting that studies the first (or base) environment, as discussed below.

14.2.1 The Base Environment

A set of environmental conditions which may be considered to form the 'base environment' then needs to be chosen. The simplest choice may be the environment to which the system most commonly interfaces. However, if such a base environment does not exist it is up to the study leader to choose an appropriate environment and define it as the base.

In the ATP example, the train travelling down the line with a single train ahead of it and no changes occurring in its interfaces to other systems along the trackside constitutes a typical environment encountered by the train. This could be used as the base environment. Nonetheless, the study leader could have taken any one of the other environments. We have often used the environment of the train in a station with the doors open.

The system is then initially studied using the normal HAZOP process, but only within the chosen base environment. Under the assumption that the environment is constant, this study examines the possible design attributes and the deviations from design intent.

During the HAZOP the team will begin to identify concerns that need to be studied in other environments. It will also note concerns that need arise as a result of the process of environmental state change. When this occurs, it is essential that the study leader (since this is a control issue) records the concerns that require to be transferred between environments in a tracking system, as outlined in Section 12.2. This is required to ensure that they are studied at the correct time and are not forgotten.

For example, in the case of the ATP, if the study were to start with the environment of the train in the station, the team might identify a number of concerns relating to the train doors being open as the train departs. The leader would note these concerns in the tracking system, explain this to the team, and then raise them again when the appropriate environment is being studied.

14.2.2 Subsequent Environments

Once the examination of the base environment is complete, a second set of environmental conditions is selected. Then, many of the ATP-environment interactions will be as in the first study, but some will have changed. The HAZOP process is carried out only on the *changed* environmental interactions, so should be more rapid than the HAZOP of the base environment.

The first step in studying this second environment is for the team to identify all the system-environment interactions that have changed. This is best done by systematically reviewing each of the interactions studied for the first environment, considering whether or not the systems to which they are linked have changed, and marking any that have on the representations being used.

For example, in the case of a study of the ATP the team could, after studying the environment of 'the train in the station with the doors open', study the ATP in the environment of 'the train in a station with the doors in the process of closing'. The ATP's changing interactions with other systems will include the interactions it has with the train doors (for example, the ATP might control the doors and also monitor the door positions so as to ensure that the train does not leave with the doors open). The interactions could also include, to a more remote degree, the passengers (since the ATP controls the doors and the passengers will have steadily reducing access to the train as the doors close). These changing interactions need to be identified and marked on the representation.

The next step is to repeat and re-examine all the deviations of the initial HAZOP for each of the system-environment changing interactions identified above, whilst allowing for the new environmental state. Using the above example, the interactions with the doors and passengers should be studied within the environment of 'the train in a station with the doors in the process of closing'.

During this re-examination, the HAZOP record of the base environment is reviewed so as to remind the team of what was previously discovered. This review also serves to help the team identify how the interactions with the environment or the behaviour of the system may deviate from what the designer expected. For example, the designer may have assumed that the change from one environment to another can occur only in one way. When the team examines the two sets of records in parallel they may realise that the change could occur in ways the designer did not allow for.

The team should then examine the deviations from design intent of all the components that are directly connected to the interactions that have changed. This is necessary in order to check for possible secondary effects, such as where a deviation in a changing interaction, while not itself having a hazardous effect, might cause deviations in the behaviour of one or more components which are hazardous.

The final step in the HAZOP process is to record the environmental interactions that have not changed between the two environments. This provides an explanation of why it is not necessary to repeat the study of a particular interaction in a particular environment.

Whilst this process is going on, the study leader has a critical control function which is to review the list of concerns noted as requiring transfer between environments and to ensure the study of those appropriate to the current environment. The study leader should mark down on the tracking system the concerns that have been covered. At the end of the HAZOP of the second environment, the study leader should review the tracking system with the team to confirm what has been done and thus build up the team's confidence in his management of this complex area.

Once the second environment has been studied a third is selected and studied, during which the records for the two previous environments are consulted. This is greatly aided by using a computer-based record of the HAZOP, which shows the relevant records.

This process is then repeated for each subsequent environment.

In the case of the ATP, the possible environments to be studied include the train travelling in the tunnel, a chosen list of potential emergency environments, the train approaching a station, the train entering the station, the train stopped with the doors closed, the doors opening, etc.

14.2.3   Examining the Process of Change Between Environments

Once all the environments have been studied, the next stage is to conduct a HAZOP of the way the system changes its environments. This is best done using a representation that describes how the environments change. A timing diagram or state transition diagram may be appropriate — see Chapter 15 for an example of this type of HAZOP. During this HAZOP the team reviews the deviations from design intent that might occur while the system is changing state.

The team must also consider how the process of change of the environment could be subject to deviations from design intent. For example, a designer might have considered that the environment will change in a particular manner, but in reality it might be capable of changing in different ways, and these need to be brought out during the study. In the ATP system, the designer might have considered that the change to the 'doors opening' environment can occur only after the train has stopped at a platform, forgetting the possibility of this change of environment occurring when the train has stopped for any number of other reasons.

Considering how the environment itself can deviate from design intent can be difficult. If a suitable representation of how the designer understood the changes of environment to occur is available (for example in a state transition diagram) a good study leader can ensure that the HAZOP examination is done in a systematic manner. In these circumstances, the HAZOP is best done by taking each step in the process of changing environmental state and postulating how it might deviate from the designer's own expectation of the way in which the environment would change.

When a deviation from the designer's expectations has been identified, the team should systematically examine the effects of that deviation on the team's previous identification of the hazards associated with the particular change of environmental state. During this process the team may then identify new hazards, or find that the previously identified hazards are more likely than they originally believed.

In the case of the ATP, if the change to the 'doors opening' environment were possible when the train stopped away from a station, a review of all the HAZOP records for the 'doors opening' environment would be required. This might then identify new hazards. For example 'passenger falls while doors open' might cause the team to identify 'passenger falls on to adjacent track' or 'passenger falls from train stopped on a bridge'.

During the HAZOP of the process of environmental change, the team will need to review the records of the hazards found in each environment, so a computer-based tool is very useful.

14.2.4   A Final Review to Check for Complete Closure

At the end of a HAZOP of this type, the final stage should involve a number of checks. These are done to ensure that the process has been completed and that no items are left unresolved.

First the study leader should 'walk' the team through all the environments and transitions that have been studied, so as to confirm what was done. This is also done to ensure that no team member has kept back a concern. For example, instead of telling the study leader, so that it could be recorded and properly tracked, a team member might have thought of a concern and made a personal note about it. Clearly this should be discouraged, but it may still occur. The 'walk through' will help remind team members of what was done and identify any concerns that were withheld.

Secondly, the study leader should review with the team all the points that were noted for transfer between environments, as previously described. This is in order to confirm that all items were addressed to the team's satisfaction.

14.3 CONCLUDING REMARKS

This chapter has examined the problems involved in studying systems that must operate within a changing environment. It suggests an approach that we have used to make the process of carrying out a HAZOP on such systems easier. The approach consists of selecting a base environment, studying it in detail and then, for subsequent environments, examining only those environmental interactions that have changed.

The chapter then went on to describe how the changes in the environment should be examined. Finally it gave guidance on how to ensure that the process described is complete.

15
Example PES HAZOP Sessions

This chapter provides two examples of small but real HAZOP sessions on computer-based systems so as to illustrate some of the points in this book. Because of the difficulty of obtaining real examples that are not commercially confidential, the material here is edited, with permission, from that given in Interim Defence Standard 00-58 [MOD 96].

Both examples use a design at the concept stage which was generated from actual work carried out by colleagues of the authors. The first example employs an automobile collision avoidance system and uses a state transition diagram as the design representation. The second uses object-oriented design representations of a helicopter engine diagnostic system.

The reader should note that, although the HAZOP sessions recorded here were real, they are included for illustration only and should not be taken to be 'perfect' studies. Each is presented in three parts:

- A description of the system using a mixture of text and the selected design representation;
- The HAZOP worksheets, as produced in real time by the HAZOP recorder, with explanations of the reasoning for some of the items;

- Some samples of typical dialogue associated with particular items discussed during the HAZOP.

15.1 COLLISION AVOIDANCE SYSTEM

15.1.1 System Description

The collision avoidance system is designed to alert the driver of a vehicle of an impending collision at low speeds. A typical situation is that of a driver of the second or third car in a queue approaching a roundabout. The driver observes the car in front starting to move off, he looks right to check clearances and moves off. The driver in front brakes, thus creating the danger of a collision.

The system comprises a radar sensor mounted centrally on the front of the car with a fan-shaped sensor beam. The geometry of the beam is such as to minimise detection of cars in adjacent lanes. The sensor system will alert the driver only when the speed is below 10 mph, as above that speed

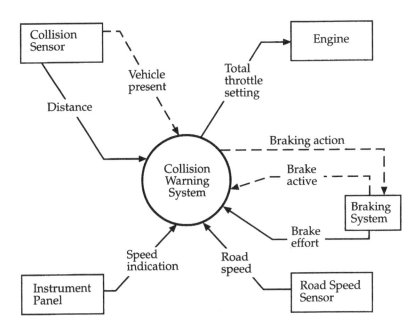

Figure 15.1: Context for the collision warning system

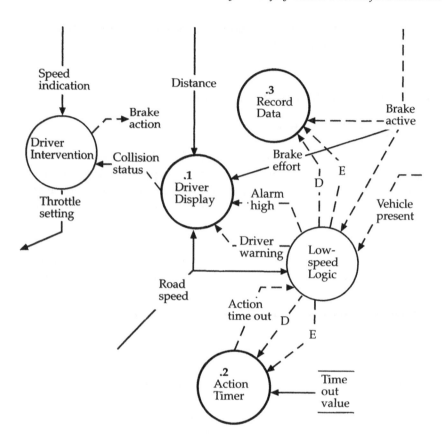

Figure 15.2: Top level decomposition for collision avoidance, showing data input to low speed logic

it is assumed that the driver will remain sufficiently far behind the car in front to be able to avoid a collision without automatic aids.

The system uses road speed, sensed from a car's normal speed sensor, and it also detects use of the brake. The system will alert the driver (by vibrating the accelerator pedal) if he is moving slowly forward (creep) and there is a vehicle in front on which he is closing. If no action is taken, then a higher level of alert is used (auditory warning). The radar system uses a series of range gates to determine the distance from the car in front. When an alert is initiated, a recorder is also activated to record car data for use in the event that a collision occurs. Figure 15.1 gives the context diagram for the complete collision avoidance system and Figure 15.2 gives the top-

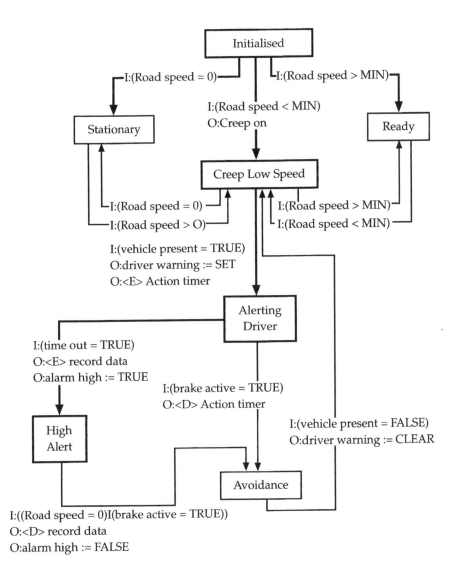

Figure 15.3: Low-speed logic state transition diagram for collision avoidance system

level decomposition showing the data input to the low-speed logic. In the latter figure, there are control flows annotated as 'D' and 'E' from 'Low-speed Logic' to 'Action Timer' and from 'Low-speed Logic' to 'Record Data', and these signify actions placed on the Action Timer and Record

Data as given in the state transition diagram. Figure 15.3 gives the state transition diagram for the low-speed logic which was chosen as the subject of the HAZOP. In the diagram the speed value MIN is given as a parameter to allow for experimentation, but we have indicated above that the recommendation for a trial implementation is to set MIN at 10 mph.

15.1.2   HAZOP Sheets for Collision Avoidance System

In this example, the guide word interpretations for the state transition diagram are those suggested in Table 7.1 of Chapter 7. The recording method used is full recording, so some of the deviations will not be credible or will have no valid meaning. Five transitions are examined, with the events triggering the transitions:

- Initialised to 'Stationary', with event: 'Road speed = 0';
- Initialised to 'Ready', with event: 'Road speed > MIN';
- Initialised to 'Creep Low Speed', with event: 'Road speed < MIN';
- 'Creep Low Speed' to 'Alerting Driver', with event: 'vehicle present = TRUE';
- 'Alerting Driver' to 'High Alert', with event: 'time out = TRUE'.

The six HAZOP sheets are given in Table 15.1, and below we go through the rationale for some of the items. With this guidance and the example dialogue given in Section 15.1.3, we hope that the interested reader will be able to follow the remainder of the items.

(a)   Items 15 and 16

Here we are looking at the event 'Road speed < MIN' and the deviation 'No' on the transition from 'Initialised' to 'Creep Low Speed'. The question is asked if it is credible that the event does not happen when it would be expected to. Clearly, this is possible and the team go on to consider the possible causes and consequences of this. Each cause/consequence combination that the team consider plausible is listed as a separate item on the HAZOP sheet. The team identify two possible causes: the first is that the road speed sensor is faulty and always reads zero (Item 15), and the second is that the road speed sensor is correct and reads zero (Item 16). For Item 15, if the deviation occurs the vehicle will enter the 'Stationary' state when it is actually moving and so the warning system will not be activated if there is a vehicle close in front. In Item 16, a design ambiguity has been revealed: what the system actually does will depend on the

Table 15.1: Example HAZOP sheets for collision avoidance (sheet 1 of 6)

HAZOP :
Diagram :   STD#94
Date :   5-Aug-94
Leader :   A Smith
Recorder :   B Smith
Team Members :   C Smith, D Jones, E Brown, F White

Collision Avoidance System

Description :

HAZOP of state transition diagram of main states of collision warning system

HAZOP item	Item	Attribute	Guide word	Cause	Consequence / implication	Indication / protection	Question / recommendation
1	Initialised to Stationary	Event 'Road speed = 0'	No	Failure of road speed sensor	No hazardous consequence		
2	Initialised to Stationary	Event 'Road speed = 0'	More		No meaning		
3	Initialised to Stationary	Event 'Road speed = 0'	Less		No meaning in this context		
4	Initialised to Stationary	Event 'Road speed = 0'	As well as	If the vehicle is stationary then the system will not be operated	Car ahead can roll back without warning		System not designed for this type of collision
5	Initialised to Stationary	Event 'Road speed = 0'	Part of		No meaning		
6	Initialised to Stationary	Event 'Road speed = 0'	Other than		No meaning		
7	Initialised to Stationary	Event 'Road speed = 0'	Early/Late		No meaning		
8	Initialised to Stationary	Event 'Road speed = 0'	Before/After		No meaning		
9	Initialised to ready	Event 'Road speed > MIN'	No		No meaning		

Table 15.1: Example HAZOP sheets for collision avoidance (sheet 2 of 6)

HAZOP item	Item	Attribute	Guide word	Cause	Consequence / implication	Indication / protection	Question / recommendation
10	Initialised to ready	Event 'Road speed > MIN'	As well as		No meaning		
11	Initialised to ready	Event 'Road speed > MIN'	Part of		No meaning		
12	Initialised to ready	Event 'Road speed > MIN'	Other than		No meaning		
13	Initialised to ready	Event 'Road speed > MIN'	Early/Late		No meaning		
14	Initialised to ready	Event 'Road speed > MIN'	Before/After		No meaning		
15	Initialised to Creep	Event 'Road speed < MIN'	No	Road speed sensor faulty	Vehicle enters Stationary mode not Creep state	Warning system not activated if there is a target	R15 Evaluate reliability of road speed sensor to determine risk of failure
16	Initialised to Creep	Event 'Road speed < MIN'	No	Road speed equals zero meeting condition for transition to both Stationary and Creep	System may be confused and choice of state will be implementation dependent		R16 Change the condition so the system has no ambiguity if Road speed = MIN
17	Initialised to Creep	Event 'Road speed < MIN'	As well as	Coasting with ignition off. Starting the engine just before the collision	Time taken to initialise the system may be insufficient to warn against collision		R17 Ensure initialisation time is in line with the preset speed and distance criteria
18	Initialised to Creep	Event 'Road speed < MIN'	As well as		No hazardous consequence		
19	Initialised to Creep	Event 'Road speed < MIN'	Other than	Sensor fault so that road speed indicated is lower than actual speed	If creep mode entered at high speed then warning signal of accelerator vibration at speed may be hazardous		R19 Consider consequences of warning system being activated at high speed e.g. while tailgating on motorway

Table 15.1: Example HAZOP sheets for collision avoidance (sheet 3 of 6)

HAZOP item	Item	Attribute	Guide word	Cause	Consequence / implication	Indication / protection	Question / recommendation
20	Initialised to Creep	Event 'Road speed < MIN'	Other than	Additional pulses leading to a false high reading of speed	Fail to go to Creep when should do		
21	Initialised to Creep	Event 'Road speed < MIN'	Other than	Wheel spin causes road speed sensor to record higher speed than actual speed	System is not activated under conditions when it is desirable for it to be		R21 Consider possible solution to provide logic to detect excessive acceleration
22	Initialised to creep	Event 'Road speed < MIN'	Early/Late	Variable time for processor to initialise			R22 Ensure the variability in initialisation of the processor, e.g. engine management system is acceptable to permit the warning system to be available promptly
23	Initialised to Creep	Event 'Road speed < MIN'	Before/After		No meaning		
24	Creep to Alerting Driver	Event vehicle present	No	Vehicle is present but system fails to detect it	Sensor may have failed		R24 Provide sensor test facility and warning light to indicate failure
25	Creep to Alerting Driver	Event vehicle present	No	Vehicle moves into lane from side. Vehicle too high to be detected			R25 Test that the sensor can detect a car entering from near side or off side and can detect the wheels on high vehicles
26	Creep to Alerting Driver	Event vehicle present	No	Target too small e.g. cyclist or motor cycle	Collision with vulnerable target not sensed		R26 Design radar sensor such that motorcycles can be detected

Table 15.1: Example HAZOP sheets for collision avoidance (sheet 4 of 6)

HAZOP item	Item	Attribute	Guide word	Cause	Consequence / implication	Indication / protection	Question / recommendation
27	Creep to Alerting Driver	Event vehicle present	Part of	A transient passage e.g. passing car or even bird initiates to alert	Transit from Alerting Driver only possible if brake pressed		R27 Filter sensor signal for transients. Consider adding an extra transition so that the alert is cancelled when the sensor signal is no longer detected for sufficient period of time e.g. a few seconds. Disable timer when Alerting Driver is left
28	Creep to Alerting Driver	Event vehicle present	Late	Filter damps reaction time of system	Crash is not avoided		R28 Investigate response profiles and braking profiles of drivers to ensure system response time is adequate
29	Creep to Alerting Driver	Event vehicle present	Late	Range gate incorrectly set or corrupted so that vehicle present = TRUE is registered too slowly. Distance registered is incorrectly interpreted as greater so that response is too slow.			R29 Investigate range gate setting so that slow response caused by corruption or false echoes is eliminated
30	Creep to Alerting Driver	Event vehicle present	As well as	Detection of distant objects as if they were near	Spurious alert		R30 The pulse repetition rate and the receive window of the sensor should be set to reduce phantom targets

Table 15.1: Example HAZOP sheets for collision avoidance (sheet 5 of 6)

HAZOP item	Item	Attribute	Guide word	Cause	Consequence / implication	Indication / protection	Question / recommendation
31	Creep to Alerting Driver	Event vehicle present	As well as	Spurious detection of mini-roundabouts, cattle grids, etc.	Spurious alerts		R31 Optimise beam geometry so as to reduce alerts from low objects
32	Creep to Alerting Driver	Event vehicle present	No	Minimum speed incorrectly set for performance of vehicle	Failure to alert		R32 Minimum value must be set according to the performance of the vehicle
33	Alerting Driver to High Alert	Event time out	No	Time out does not occur	No data is recorded and crash occurs without high alert		R33 Time out depends on driver response time which needs to be very fast. Consider if High Alert serves a practical purpose. Consider initiating data recording at Alerting Driver
34	Alerting Driver to High Alert	Event time out	Early	Time out too quick and so system enters High Alert immediately after Alerting Driver	Driver starts to ignore warnings		R34 Verify timing is adjusted so that rapid transit to High Alert does not occur
35	Alerting Driver to High Alert	Event time out	As well as	Target vanishes, for example accelerates after High Alert instigated	No exit path other than braking		R35 Consider Target false exit from High Alert with a time out on it
36	Alerting Driver to High Alert	Event time out	Part of		No meaning		
37	Alerting Driver to High Alert	Event time out	Other than	If Brake active = TRUE occurs with Time out = TRUE action is unclear	Outcome will be implementation dependant		R37 Brake active = TRUE should have priority over Time out = TRUE

Table 15.1: Example HAZOP sheets for collision avoidance (sheet 6 of 6)

HAZOP item	Item	Attribute	Guide word	Cause	Consequence / implication	Indication / protection	Question / recommendation
38	Alerting Driver to High Alert	Event time out	Early/ Late	The time interval on the timer is important. If this is long in relation to the response time of the driver the recording sequence may not be initiated			R38 If implementation is a cyclic process the timing of the cycle should be investigated to ensure that it is compatible with response time required of the driver and system
39	Alerting Driver to High Alert	Event time out	Before/ After		Not applicable		

detailed implementation — so there is a recommendation to change the design so that the speed must be both greater than zero and less than MIN for the event to be triggered.

(b)   Items 19, 20 and 21

Here we look at the same event as in Items 15 and 16, but we consider the deviation 'Other than'. The deviation is considered credible, and the team considers its possible causes and the consequences. Three situations are identified:

- There is a sensor fault, so that a vehicle travelling faster than speed MIN is indicated to be travelling at less than speed MIN, thus triggering the transition to the 'Creep Low Speed' mode. If the driver is close behind another car, the warning system may be activated (by vibrating the accelerator pedal) and the driver may be confused (Item 19).
- There is the opposite situation of extra sensor pulses leading to an erroneously high reading of speed so that the system does not transit to the 'Creep Low Speed' state when it should, and the warning system will not be activated in circumstances when it should be (Item 20).
- A full description of Item 21 is given in the example dialogue in Section 15.1.3.

(c)   Item 34

This item considers the transition from 'Alerting Driver' to 'High Alert', the event is 'time out = TRUE' and the deviation considered is 'Early'. The team judges this to be a credible deviation and then goes on to consider possible causes and consequences. The deviation can occur if the timer is set incorrectly. As a result, the time-out occurs too soon after the transition to 'Alerting Driver', and the 'High Alert' state is entered and an audible warning sounded. If this happens consistently, the driver may start to ignore the warnings, with an increased risk of collision. A recommendation is made to adjust the timing so that an over-rapid transit to 'High Alert' will not happen.

(d)   Item 37

This item considers the same event as Item 34 but examines the deviation 'Other than'. Again it is considered credible that some confusion could occur with other events. A cause is identified: if 'Brake active = TRUE' occurs at the same time as 'Time out = TRUE' then it is not clear what the expected action should be and there may be a transition to 'High Alert' or to 'Avoidance' depending on the details of the implementation. A recommendation is made for the event 'Brake active = TRUE' to take precedence over 'Time out = TRUE'.

15.1.3   Example Dialogues from HAZOP Session

Section 15.1.2 gave an explanation of some of the HAZOP items shown in Table 15.1 but no indication of the interaction between team members that occurred during the process of the study. Here we give two example dialogues taken from the HAZOP session which give an idea of how the team members interacted and worked together to come to their conclusions.

(a)   Example Dialogue 1 — Item 21

Leader: Consider the system moving from the state 'Initialised' to state 'Creep Low Speed', the event attribute 'Road speed < MIN', and the deviation 'Other than'. How can we have other things happening on this event?

Member: What happens if you pull out and get into a wheel spin?

Designer: The road speed sensor could think that the vehicle is moving a lot faster than it actually is, as it measures from the wheels.

Member: So the system may not be activated when it was designed to be because it could think that the vehicle was going faster than speed MIN?

Designer: Yes, the system will only work below speed MIN.

Leader: So this is a hazard which needs to be recorded?

Designer: Yes, the system needs to measure the rate of acceleration, and if this is too large it needs to compensate for it when measuring the road speed.

Leader: Let's not work out details of the solution now, but record it as a hazard and recommend that potential solutions be explored, noting the suggestion just made.

(b)   Example Dialogue 2 — Item 26

Leader: In looking at the system moving from state 'Creep Low Speed' to state 'Alerting Driver', and considering the event 'Vehicle present = TRUE', we have already identified two possible causes of the deviation 'No'. Are there any others?

Member: What range has the radar sensor got?

Designer: It is designed to pick up a vehicle directly ahead, the coverage and range is one lane's width at 20 metres.

Member: Would it pick up a small target such as a bike?

Designer: Yes, it is sensitive enough to do so if it is directly ahead.

Leader: What about a motorbike which was at the side of the vehicle and just ahead?

Designer: I suppose it could be missed. The system would then not warn the driver of the motorbike's presence, as the condition for move into the 'Alerting Driver' state requires 'Vehicle present = TRUE'.

Leader: That sounds like a major hazard. Let's recommend that the design of the radar sensor be evaluated with a view to aiding detection.

15.2 HELICOPTER ON-BOARD DIAGNOSTICS

The application concerns a computer-based system for on-board fault diagnosis in a helicopter. Various events and symptoms (pieces of 'evidence') occur, and information about them is derived from instrument readings or pilot actions. The information is used by the computer-based system to reason about the state of the helicopter and to identify faults. The computer system notifies faults to the pilot by highlighting a fault central warning panel (FCWP) and displaying a text description of the fault. If a fault is suspected but not unambiguously identified, then a warning panel is highlighted. Sometimes the system may have a hypothesis for the diagnosis but need additional information: it may then ask the pilot to perform some actions that will provide additional information to assist in the diagnosis. Some actions might be recommended as a consequence of a completed diagnosis; for example, 'Land as soon as practicable'. The pilot can ask for the explanation of a fault by clicking on the FCWP.

15.2.1   Description of the Design

An object oriented design is chosen as the means of representing the system. Object orientation divides up the functionality required of a system according to the types of entity which have been identified in the system (note that 'entity' in this chapter has its object oriented meaning as described in Chapter 7). Data structures and (parts of) function definitions are combined into the definition of a 'class', which acts as a template for creating 'instances'. An object is a module that combines state information with processing capability.

The terms used to describe the basics of object orientation vary with the particular style of representation chosen. The state information is held in 'instance variables', or 'attributes', or 'slots'; the processing capability is provided in 'methods', or 'operations', and so on. An object does not, strictly speaking, directly access the data or invoke the functions of another object. Instead it 'sends a message' to another object naming the information or processing that is required. Details of how the information or the processing is provided are hidden, leading to a more modular implementation that is relatively easy to revise. The example given here uses the Shlaer-Mellor conventions for representation.

The Shlaer-Mellor approach to object oriented development consists of two activities [Shlaer 92]:

- Object oriented analysis (OOA);
- A technique for object oriented design (OOD) called 'recursive design' (RD).

The OOA activity produces different types of model, as described in Chapter 7:

- Information models, describing objects, their attributes and their relationships;
- State models, consisting of state machine descriptions of object life cycles;
- Object communication models, exhibiting the asynchronous communication between objects;
- Object access models, exhibiting the synchronous communication between objects.

In addition there are often process models consisting of data flow diagrams detailing object actions.

The OOD activity consists largely of defining classes implementable from objects identified in the OOA. A specific design language is used to describe four types of model:

- Inheritance diagrams;
- Dependency diagrams;
- Class diagrams;
- Class structure charts.

(a)   *Introduction to the Design Description*

Describing the design of the helicopter fault diagnosis system in the detailed design language would produce a representation which is too complicated for the purposes of the example HAZOP. Instead, simplified versions of class diagrams and dependency diagrams have been produced. (The design does not exploit inheritance relations, so the inheritance diagrams are not relevant, while accurate class structure charts would be too complicated for the purpose of the HAZOP.)

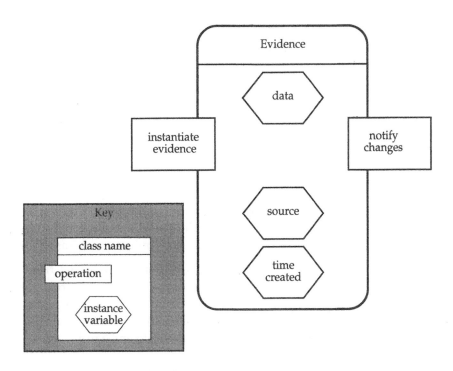

Figure 15.4: Object oriented design notation example

(b)   Classes

Figure 15.4 shows both the design notation used for class diagrams and an example of the key evidence class:

- Hexagons indicate object attributes or state variables ('instance variables'). In the example, the data is associated with the source of the data and the time the data was created.
- Oblongs indicate operations which the object can perform. In the example, there are operations to instantiate the evidence and to provide notification of changes.

(c)   Dependencies and Connections

Figure 15.5 is a top-level view of the system, showing the connections between the objects. The computer-based system is inside the inner box. The objects Helicopter, Pilot and Developer are viewed as external objects, or objects of another domain.

     The object connections are of three types:

- Invoking an operation on another object, where the invocation (given the current implementation) involves a transfer of control;
- Accessing the attribute values of another object;
- Sending a message to an object, where the receiving object treats the message as an event to be dealt with at a later date.

Figure 15.5 shows the message connections between objects and also can be considered a dependency diagram, as described in [Shlaer 92].

(d)   Detailed Interactions

Figure 15.6 elaborates on part of the picture contained in the top-level diagram. It shows the operations used by the classes involved in the object connections on which the HAZOP focused. The conventions are as follows:

- Invocation of an object operation is shown by an arrow from an operation of one object to that of another (for example, from 'send value' to 'store value');
- An access to an object, which requires a result to be returned, is shown with bi-directional arrows (for example, from 'handle value' to 'instantiate evidence');
- A dotted line indicates an operation that generates an event to which the target object eventually responds with the target operation (for

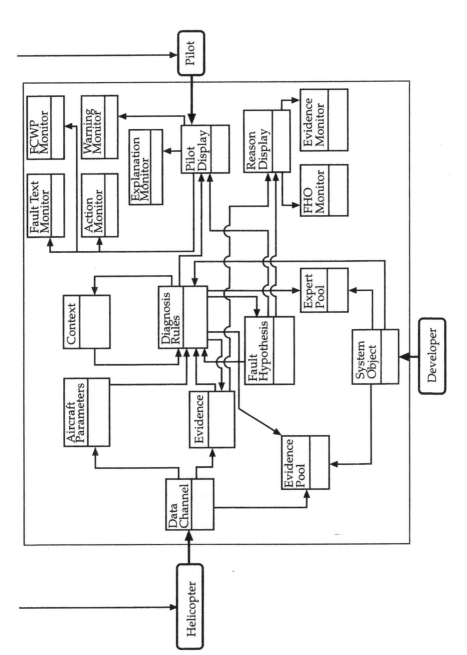

Figure 15.5: Top-level view of the helicopter on-board system

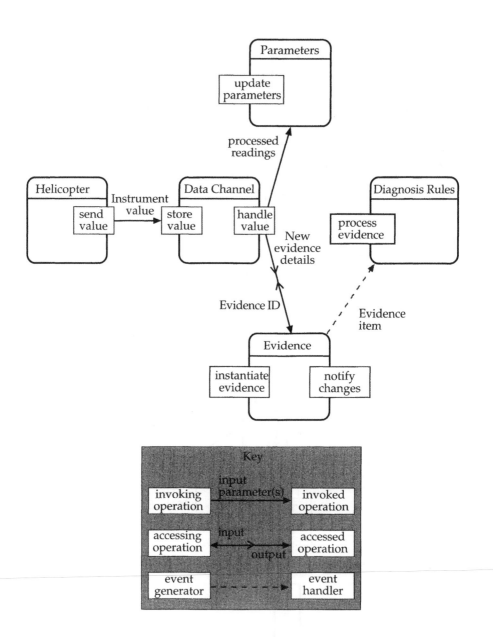

Figure 15.6: Part of the on-board system in more detail

example, 'notify changes' to 'process evidence');

- Arrows are given a label which names the parameter, or group of parameters, passing between the objects (for example, 'instrument value' between 'send value' and 'store value').

(e)   Intended Operation of the System

The following describes the roles of the objects in producing the behaviour of the system. In Figure 15.5 the names of the object classes are capitalised. The example HAZOP analysis concentrated on a small number of connections between objects (see Figure 15.6). For those connections, the operations are indicated in *italics*.

i)   The external Helicopter object sends instrument readings and status reports (*send_value*) into the fault diagnosis system to be received by the Data Channel objects (*store_value*).

ii)   The Data Channel object responds to these values (with *handle_value*) by:

   —   Updating the internal description of the helicopter (Aircraft Parameters with *update_parameters*);
   —   Arranging for the creation of a piece of evidence (Evidence, with *instantiate_evidence*, which returns an object reference);
   —   Arranging for a new piece of evidence to be posted where it is visible (in Evidence Pool).

iii) The Context object provides an extra layer of control to the diagnosis process.

iv)   The Aircraft Parameters object tells (*notify_changes*) the Diagnosis Rules object of the changes it has handled.

v)   The Evidence object tells (*notify_changes*) the Diagnosis Rules object of the piece of evidence it has constructed.

vi)   The Diagnosis Rules object performs the diagnostic reasoning. It responds to the reported changes with its processing operations (for example, *process_evidence*). This response is enabled by an event from the System Object invoking the *run* operation on Diagnosis Rules). It results in a complex operation which invokes further operations on many other objects:

   —   A new 'control record' (Context) may be created;
   —   The 'control record' may be switched;
   —   Evidence may be created (Evidence, with *instantiate_evidence*,

    returns an object reference);

— Evidence may be associated with a fault hypothesis;
— Evidence may be posted (into Evidence Pool);
— A new fault diagnosis record (Fault Hypothesis) may be created;
— The fault diagnosis record may be updated;
— A fault hypothesis record may incorporate new evidence;
— A request for pilot action might be displayed (on Pilot Display);
— A diagnosis record may be posted (into Expert Pool).

vii) The Fault Hypothesis object records the progress of the diagnosis. It invokes operations on Reason Display and Pilot Display to display information on the record, and feeds back changes to the record into Diagnosis Rules.

viii) The Pilot Display takes the parameters passed by Diagnosis Rules or Fault Hypothesis when they invoke its operations. It also handles events deriving from actions by the (external) Pilot object. It analyses the messages it receives, divides the parameters it receives and sends different parts to appropriate displays:

— Fault Text Monitor handles the text underneath the 'Fault' caption;
— Action Monitor handles the text underneath the 'Actions' caption;
— FCWP Monitor controls the highlighting of fault indicators
— Warning Monitor controls the highlighting of the Warning strip;
— Explanation Monitor handles the EXPLAIN indicator and the text underneath the Explanation caption.

ix) The Reason Display takes the parameters passed by Evidence and Fault Hypothesis when they invoke its operations. It analyses the messages it receives, divides the parameters received, and sends different parts to appropriate displays.

x) The Expert Pool object acts as an area where the Diagnosis Rules object posts information on the diagnosis record.

xi) The Evidence Pool object acts as an area where the Data Channel and Diagnosis Rules objects post information on pieces of evidence.

xii) The System Object responds to an instruction from the (external) Developer object, invokes operations on Evidence Pool and Expert Pool to check for changes in those data areas, and enables the Diagnosis Rules object.

15.2.2 HAZOP Sheets for Helicopter On-board Diagnostics

The seven HAZOP sheets in Table 15.2 address three data flows that are shown in Figure 15.6:

- The data flow of 'instrument value' from the invoking operation 'send value' in the object class 'Helicopter' to the invoked operation 'store value' in the object class 'Data Channel';
- The data flow 'new evidence details' from the accessing operation 'handle value' in the object class 'Data Channel' to the accessed operation 'instantiate evidence' in the object class 'Evidence';
- The data flow 'evidence item' from the event generator 'notify changes' in the object class 'Evidence' to the event handler 'process evidence' in the object class 'Diagnosis Rules'.

The guide word interpretations used are those given in Table 7.1 for data flow. The HAZOP sheets are given in Table 15.2 and the recording method used is exception recording. As for the collision avoidance example given in Section 15.1, below we go through the rationale for some of the items. With this guidance and the example dialogues given in Section 15.2.3, we hope that the interested reader will be able to follow the remainder of the items in Table 15.2.

(a) Items 3, 4, 5 and 6

Here we are looking at the first of the data flows described above, that of 'instrument value' and the deviation 'other than' which Table 7.1 interprets in this context as 'information complete but incorrect'. The team first consider whether such a deviation is credible and there is an obvious consensus that it is. The team then go on to consider the possible causes and consequences and four cases are identified:

- A value may be received that is outside the credible range. The designer states that some of the data is checked within 'Data Channel' but is not sure that all critical sensor values are checked in this way. The team agree that an incorrect diagnosis might result from an out-of-range value and recommend that all critical sensor values should be subjected to a plausibility check (Item 3).
- A value in the valid range may still be incorrect and it is unlikely to be trapped by the range plausibility checks recommended for Item 3. The result, again, may be an incorrect diagnosis. The team recommend that checks be considered to identify sudden changes in

Table 15.2: Example HAZOP sheets for helicopter diagnosis (sheet 1 of 7)

HAZOP :

Diagram : Helicopter Fault Warning System

Date : Figure 15.6

Leader : 11-Aug-94

Recorder : ABC

Team Members : XYZ

Z, Z2, Z3, Z4

Description : HAZOP of object oriented design for a fault warning system for helicopter pilots.

HAZOP item	Item	Attribute	Guide word	Cause	Consequence / implication	Indication / protection	Question / recommendation	Answers / comments
1	Helicopter send value to Data Channel store value	Data flow	No	Failure of send value method or instrument sensor	System will not know that this has occurred and may make misdiagnosis, fail to diagnose fault etc. as it will not receive updated values		R1 Means should be provided to warn the pilot that the system is not receiving the instrumental values it requires to function as designed	
2	Helicopter send value to Data Channel store value	Data flow	As well as	Other interference from the operating environment	Data values are corrupted by interference		R2 This is beyond the scope of this particular study, but it is recommended that it be examined in another study	
3	Helicopter send value to Data Channel store value	Data flow	Other than	Value is received in the correct form but is incorrect value i.e. out of range	Diagnosis may be based on incorrect values	Some data is checked within Data Channel to ensure it is within legal values (plausibility check)	R3 Ensure that all critical sensor values are included in the plausibility check	

Table 15.2: Example HAZOP sheets for helicopter diagnosis (sheet 2 of 7)

HAZOP item	Item	Attribute	Guide word	Cause	Consequence / implication	Indication / protection	Question / recommendation	Answers / comments
4	Helicopter send value to Data Channel store value	Data flow	Other than	A value is received which is in the valid range but is incorrect	Diagnosis may be made based on incorrect data	Plausibility checks will not realise that this data is erroneous	R4 Consider checks to eliminate spurious changes, for example, a rate of data change check	
5	Helicopter send value to Data Channel store value	Data flow	Other than	Corruption in the Data Channel reference	The correct value may be sent to the wrong object. If there is a permanent change in reference this would lead to loss of data	Recommendations 3 and 4 would help prevent incorrect data being used. Recommendation 1 would help if no data were sent	N5 See previous recommendations R1, R3 and R4	
6	Helicopter send value to Data Channel store value	Data flow	Other than	Helicopter may not have checks on the data which is sent to the system	Erroneous data may be passed to the system		R6 Carry out a study to identify the safety-critical aspects of the sensor values and to ensure an adequate degree of integrity of sensor and Data Channel	
7	Helicopter send value to Data Channel store value	Data flow	Before/After	Incorrect sequencing of data values received	System will use incorrect evidence in making diagnoses		R7 Data sequencing should be considered as part of the study carried out under R6	

Table 15.2: Example HAZOP sheets for helicopter diagnosis (sheet 3 of 7)

HAZOP item	Item	Attribute	Guide word	Cause	Consequence / implication	Indication / protection	Question / recommendation	Answers / comments
8	Helicopter send value to Data Channel store value	Data rate	More	Data rate is too high	Data items may be missed and so system may make diagnosis based on out of date data		R8 Consider incorporating data rate verification and warning in Data Channel object, and also include data synchronisation in helicopter study under R6	
9	Helicopter send value to Data Channel store value	Data rate	More	Rate of data input is too high	Data store becomes full, system would not be able to process new values and diagnosis would become out of date	System is designed to keep on reasoning with available data	R9 A study should be conducted to determine the implications of each fault on helicopter safety and the consequences of late or missing diagnoses. The system should issue a warning to the pilot if this occurs	
10	Data Channel handle value to instantiate evidence	Data flow	No	Failure of the handle value method	No evidence created so no or incorrect diagnosis will be made	Relies on the integrity of the code	R10 The handle value code should be subject to sufficient verification and validation	

Table 15.2: Example HAZOP sheets for helicopter diagnosis (sheet 4 of 7)

HAZOP item	Item	Attribute	Guide word	Cause	Consequence / implication	Indication / protection	Question / recommendation	Answers / comments
11	Data Channel handle value to instantiate evidence	Data flow	All deviations	Failure of the handle value method	Integrity of code in handle value method in Data Channel object is key for a correct diagnosis		R11 A safety-critical method and assessment should be used in the development of handle value method. See R10	
12	Data Channel handle value to instantiate evidence	Data flow	Other than	Incorrect implementation of the rules for designating values as evidence. These rules are fixed in the system	New evidence details are not recognised and transmitted		R12 When handle value code is implemented, consider how to validate the parameters that are used to define what is new evidence	
13	Data Channel handle value to instantiate evidence	Data rate	More	Evidence is passed at too high a rate	System may become overwhelmed and fall over		N13 The rate of new evidence updating is not considered likely to overwhelm the fault diagnosis: the critical rate is set by information received from the helicopter	
14	Data Channel handle value to instantiate evidence	Data flow	No	Lack of pilot action or failure of handle value to generate new evidence	System will wait for action or evidence		R14 Provide time-out on pilot actions and indication if evidence has not changed	

Table 15.2: Example HAZOP sheets for helicopter diagnosis (sheet 5 of 7)

HAZOP item	Item	Attribute	Guide word	Cause	Consequence / implication	Indication / protection	Question / recommendation	Answers / comments
15	Data Channel handle value to instantiate evidence	Data flow	Part of	Generation of messages is event driven and so evidence might be missed	Algorithms fail to recognise a critical event		R15 The criticality of evidence should be considered and critical evidence should be sent repetitively	
16	Data Channel handle value to instantiate evidence	Data flow	Before / After	Handle value passes values to some but not all objects (should pass values to Aircraft Parameters, Evidence and Evidence Pool)	Data is not current in all objects and a misdiagnosis may be possible as there is missing or incorrect data, or Diagnosis Rules is not told to take action		R16 Implementation of handle value must be verified to ensure the correct sequence, i.e. instantiate evidence before adding evidence	
17	Data Channel handle value to update parameters	Data flow	After	New evidence was notified to evidence pool but Aircraft Parameters were not updated in time	Diagnosis Rules will begin to process with incorrect values risking incorrect diagnosis		R17 Consider ways to check that Aircraft Parameters have been updated when new evidence is entered into evidence pool	
18	Data Channel handle value to update parameters	Data flow	No	Old parameters in Aircraft Parameters have not been updated and are sent to Diagnosis Rules	An inappropriate hypothesis may be generated		R18 See previous recommendation R17	

Table 15.2: Example HAZOP sheets for helicopter diagnosis (sheet 6 of 7)

HAZOP item	Item	Attribute	Guide word	Cause	Consequence / implication	Indication / protection	Question / recommendation	Answers / comments
19	Data Channel handle value to instantiate evidence	Data flow	Other than	Incorrect object reference returned by instantiate evidence	Incorrect object reference is associated with Evidence		R19 Code for instantiate evidence should be subject to appropriate verification and validation	
20	Evidence notify changes to Diagnosis Rules	Data flow	No	Evidence change details are not passed to Diagnosis Rules	Diagnostic Rules not updated	If evidence relates to a potentially hazardous situation it will not be communicated	R20 Apply checks within Diagnostic Rules to check that Evidence and Aircraft Parameters are consistent, and to take appropriate action if they are not	
21	Evidence notify changes to Diagnosis Rules	Data flow	Other than	Details relating to an incorrect evidence item are passed	Diagnostic Rules may produce a false diagnosis which could be hazardous		R21 See previous recommendation R20	
22	Evidence notify changes to Diagnosis Rules	Data flow	Other than	Incompatibility between the evidence that is notified and the new parameter that is notified	Diagnosis Rules may produce a false diagnosis which could be dangerous		R22 See previous recommendation R20	
23	Evidence notify changes to Diagnosis Rules	Data flow	After	Evidence objects queue for processing. Aircraft Parameters updated more rapidly	Evidence and Aircraft Parameters would be inconsistent		N23 Data rate is sufficiently slow to prevent too large a queue forming	

Table 15.2: Example HAZOP sheets for helicopter diagnosis (sheet 7 of 7)

HAZOP item	Item	Attribute	Guide word	Cause	Consequence / implication	Indication / protection	Question / recommendation	Answers / comments
24	Evidence notify change to Diagnosis Rules	Data flow	Other than	Problem of synchronising evidence and Aircraft Parameters as previously, or due to spurious evidence	A hypothesis is rejected on false evidence. The system will then not be able to reconsider this hypothesis if new evidence is received and may be unable to reach a conclusion		R24 Consider means by which Diagnosis Rules can recover a discarded hypothesis if new evidence is received	
25	Evidence notify changes to Diagnosis Rules	Data flow	Other than	Diagnosis Rules considers it has made a diagnosis and awaits pilot action when new evidence discounting hypothesis is received	New evidence is ignored		Q25 Is Diagnosis Rules able to process new information after diagnosis has reached a completed stage?	A25 System will start a new diagnosis. This may lead to a new fault with new actions being requested. Consider implications on pilot confidence

data (Item 4).

- It is identified that if the data channel reference is corrupted then the correct value may be sent to the wrong object, resulting in a loss of data. The team identify that the recommendations on Items 3 and 4 would help prevent incorrect data being used. If the fault is persistent then the recommendation of Item 1 to warn the pilot that there is a data fault is relevant (Item 5).
- The team identify that the helicopter object may send incorrect data because it is not checked before sending and, as in the above items, this could result in an incorrect diagnosis. The team recommend that a study be done on the safety-critical aspects of the data values (Item 6).

(b)   Items 8 and 9

As for the items above, the same data flow is examined, but this time the attribute considered is 'data rate' and the deviation is 'more', interpreted as 'the data rate is too high'. The team consider that this is credible and go on to explore the possible causes and consequences. The team identify the following:

- There is a danger that some data items may not be received, and this may result in a diagnosis that is made on out-of-date data. The team make recommendations to build in checks of data rate (Item 8).
- Another result of the deviation is that the data store might become full, new values would not be processed and the diagnosis would be out of date. The designer says that the system will keep on reasoning with whatever data is available in the store. The team recommend a study to check the implications of such faults on helicopter safety (Item 9).

(c)   Item 15

This item looks at the data flow from 'handle value' to 'instantiate evidence' and the deviation 'part of', interpreted as 'the information passed is incomplete'. The team believe this is a credible deviation and consider the causes and consequences. The designer states that the generation of messages is event driven, so some evidence might be missed. The result could be that the algorithms fail to recognise a critical event. The team recommend that evidence is ranked depending on its criticality and the most critical should be sent repeatedly.

(d)   Item 20

This item looks at the data flow from 'notify changes' to 'process evidence' and the deviation 'no' (with the obvious interpretation of 'no data passed'). The team consider that the deviation is credible. As a result of no evidence being passed, the evidence is not updated, and if it relates to a potentially hazardous situation, it could result in no warning being given to the pilot. The team recommend that checks are carried out to ensure that evidence is consistent with aircraft parameters and that appropriate action should be taken if they are not.

   Note that when a possible hazard is identified, the team do not spend time working on design solutions. However, when their combined experience suggests a clear way forward they will note it and recommend that it should be considered. Often, the recommendation is to carry out a specific study.

15.2.3   Example Dialogues from the HAZOP

Section 15.2.2 gave an explanation of some of the HAZOP items shown in Table 15.2 but it did not offer any indication of the interaction between team members that occurred while the study was being carried out. We now give two example dialogues, taken from the HAZOP session, to show how the team members interacted and worked together in arriving at their conclusions.

(a)   Example Dialogue 1 — Item 2

Leader: Consider the data flow between Helicopter 'send value' method and Data Channel 'store value' method, and consider the deviation 'As well as'. How can we get other information in this data flow?

Member: From the helicopter, via any interference from outside the system.

Member: Do we know anything about that, for example, would the system be protected against it?

Designer: No, the data may become corrupted by interference, which could cause the system to malfunction.

Leader: Would the interference be caused by something within the system or external to the system?

Designer: External to the system in this case, for example, other parts of the helicopter.

Leader: Then we need not go into detail about the causes or solution to these factors as they are outside the scope of this study. Let's record that they should be investigated and move on.

Designer: Recommend that a further study should be carried out as I think this is important to the system.

Leader: Yes, we should add that.

(b)   Example Dialogue 2 — Item 23

Leader   Consider the data flow from Evidence 'notify changes' method to 'process evidence' in Diagnosis Rules, and consider the deviation 'After'. How can this happen?

Member: If there is a lot of evidence what does the system do?

Designer: The evidence items would be placed in a queue for processing.

Member: What if aircraft parameters are updated while evidence data is queuing?

Member: Is it possible that the system will work with inconsistent data if it is using more up-to-date aircraft parameters than evidence?

Leader: Shall we record that as a hazard then?

Designer: No, the system may act incorrectly if this occurs, but the data rate of evidence is fairly slow so I can't conceive of how a large queue would form that could not be processed in time. I don't think it will happen in practice.

Leader: OK, we'll just record a note that we discussed it and then move on.

15.3   CONCLUDING REMARKS

This chapter has offered two practical examples of HAZOPs. The HAZOP worksheets were shown and sample items from them explained. In addition, paraphrased dialogues from four items discussed at the study sessions were presented. It is hoped that after studying these examples readers will be able to use their understanding of them to deduce how the other conclusions on the worksheets were arrived at.

The sample dialogues also offer a feel for the balance between allowing sufficient focused discussion for arriving at sensible conclusions and excluding diversionary discussion which would render the meeting inefficient.

16

Introduction, Auditing and Improvement of HAZOP

In the previous chapters, the importance of good management of HAZOP has continually been emphasised, with guidelines and procedures being given for controlling the study process. This chapter too is concerned with management issues, but not with the management of the HAZOP process itself; rather, the focus here is on three other issues:

- Introducing HAZOP into an organisation;
- Auditing HAZOP;
- Improving the effectiveness and efficiency of HAZOP.

16.1 INTRODUCING HAZOP INTO AN ORGANISATION

Introducing a technique such as HAZOP into an organisation presupposes a readiness within the organisation to accept and use it. If there is not such a readiness, the technique is unlikely to be received enthusiastically or used when it should be, and likely to be employed inefficiently and ineffectively when it is used.

On the face of it, the HAZOP process is not difficult to carry out. Its operational principles are easy to understand, and those using it may gain the impression that if a team reviews a design from the point of view of safety, using an approach with similar operational principles to those of HAZOP, the job has been done. This apparent simplicity can lead to the ineffectiveness and inefficiency of many studies — for reasons such as: the study leader has been unwisely chosen, the study has been inadequately planned and controlled, or the team has been incompetently led. But worse, the failure of the process to achieve the desired results has often been attributed to shortcomings in HAZOP itself rather than to the way in which it was conducted. The benefits which the process could offer in the future are then lost.

So, we should ask, 'How can it be ensured that the introduction of HAZOP is successful and that the technique is employed to the benefit of the organisation?' There is no single action which will guarantee success; a number of components need to converge.

16.1.1   Knowledgeable Management and Leadership

If HAZOP is to be introduced into our organisation, when and under what circumstances should it be used? Should its use be mandatory or discretionary? Conceptually, it seems easy to carry out, so do we really have to adhere to its rules? What will happen if we don't? And who would find out, anyway? These questions show that there is more to introducing HAZOP than training a few people and telling them to get on with it (see [Redmill 88a]). What is more, they reveal two aspects of the introduction: the strategic and the tactical.

Strategically, it has to be decided when HAZOP should be used within the organisation — for example, in given types of projects, when certain types of objectives need to be met, or, perhaps, in all instances when safety is an issue. Senior management must decide. Once the decision has been made, it needs to be communicated to all relevant personnel and documented in the organisation's standards and procedures. Further, to ensure that the strategic requirements are adhered to, the responsibility for initiating and monitoring HAZOP in each instance needs to be clearly defined (see Chapter 5).

In order to create plans for the strategic application of HAZOP, management needs to understand the difficulties of applying the technique as well as its potential, and to have well-defined objectives for what they expect of it. They must also be alert to the need for strategic plans for the technique's use, and they must recognise that without a properly defined strategy HAZOP would almost certainly fall into disrepute, having failed to reveal its benefits. Further, management needs to monitor the application of HAZOP over a lengthy period (at least a year) to ensure that the strategy is being adhered to, that the defined responsibilities are understood and are being discharged, and that the technique is being applied in all relevant instances.

Then there is the tactical side of the introduction of HAZOP. Not only should it be decreed that the technique is to be used, but the details of its use must also be defined, communicated and monitored. For example, meeting rules similar to those in Chapter 9 should be set and adhered to — such rules are defined not arbitrarily but for the purpose of maximising the effectiveness and efficiency of the technique. It is easy for a study leader, particularly one who is substandard and who has not achieved as much as he or she had hoped to do in a meeting, to contemplate extending the meeting's duration. Only if management has clearly laid down the rules, convinced people to observe them, and put a process of monitoring in place, will the temptation consistently be resisted. Nor does monitoring necessarily need to be carried out at the meeting itself; it may be done subsequently, from the meeting records, which should carry all meeting details, including the start and finish times.

Defining the strategy for the introduction of HAZOP and the tactical rules for its use must be done at a sufficiently high level in the organisation. Subsequently, senior management must be seen to take an interest in the success of the technique. To ask participants, 'Do you find that HAZOP is delivering what you want from it?' or 'How did the study go?' or 'Was this study any easier that the one before?' is to show that you are interested and thus to keep others interested too. Management also needs to be seen to be concerned about the improvement of the use of the technique, so when results suggest inefficiencies, or a declining trend, they should enquire about the reasons and what could be done to improve things. If they are perceived to remain remote from the application of the technique, especially when participants know that it is not being used successfully, HAZOP will be discredited.

16.1.2   Having a Champion

It is always an advantage to have a 'champion' to facilitate the introduction of something new. In this case, a champion is someone who knows and understands HAZOP, is convinced of its benefits, proclaims its virtues, and is active in helping to promote and facilitate its introduction.

If the initial stage of the introduction is effectively carried out by management, it is often the case that a champion emerges — someone who immediately recognises the benefits of the technique and wants it to be used as soon as possible in all appropriate cases. But a champion needs to be chosen and used with care. It is important that the champion should not only appreciate HAZOP because it discovers hazards, but also recognise the reasons why it does so, which are based on its formality and the control of the process. The champion, in advocating HAZOP, needs to emphasise the importance of using it properly rather than merely of using it. In cases where the role of the champion has led to later problems, the champion has been an enthusiast who has not cared for rules, and this has led to uncontrolled practices.

It is important for management not merely to let enthusiasts loose to introduce HAZOP in their own way, but to ensure that they are the right people for the job, that they have the right motives, and that they are fully trained in using and teaching the technique. Even then, management needs to monitor the activities of champions, for champions in their enthusiasm can be too concerned for others to be like them and share their perceptions, and this can deter rather than attract prospective proponents of HAZOP.

Nevertheless, a champion can be a great asset to the introduction of HAZOP, and management would do well to find, train, and encourage such a person — and then to monitor their activities to ensure that the formalities of the process are not being overlooked, or circumvented.

16.1.3   Training

Typically, management recognises the need for training in new techniques. But it has not been uncommon for study leaders to receive no HAZOP training — for two main reasons. The first is that the technique seems so easy to apply that management believe that any intelligent person could lead a study. The second is that the means of training may not be obvious.

But training for the study leader is essential, particularly as the role of study leader is so crucial to the harmony and productivity of the study team, the success of the study, and the costs borne by the organisation.

(See Section 6.4.2 for advice on training.) Consider this: a study which should take six 3-hour meetings takes eight because of the study leader's lack of control. This is a 33% excess and, with six team members, it represents a waste of 36 person-hours. Multiply this inefficiency over a number of studies, and it becomes obvious that stinting on training is false economy. Moreover, if the meeting is inefficient, it is likely also to be ineffective — i.e. it will not find all the hazards that it should. So, as well as employing an excess of time, the route may already be open for later breaches of system safety.

An organisation should conduct short in-house sessions, at least to inform study leaders of:

- Local rules, standards and procedures;
- Their various responsibilities;
- What authority is invested in them.

Then, on-the-job training should be provided, as recommended in Section 6.4.2.

The question of the authority of study leaders is often overlooked, and this can have significant effects. For example, it was stated in Chapter 9 that if efficiency or effectiveness lapses too severely, the study leader should stop the study. Unless the study leaders are confident that senior management will be supportive of such an action, they may be afraid or reluctant to take it — with the result of continued failure of the technique.

16.1.4   Safety Management System

The place of HAZOP in safety analysis was explained in Chapter 2. A good HAZOP is invaluable whenever safety is an issue, but the results are used to best effect only within a process of safety analysis which continues throughout the life of the system in question. Further, it is now accepted that the disciplines imposed by a safety management system are essential to maintaining the impetus of a continuing safety analysis.

Although HAZOP may bring benefits on its own, it is more likely to do so if it is introduced as an integral part of a safety management system which provides the infrastructure for mitigating identified hazards. If such a system does not already exist, it needs to be introduced at the same time as HAZOP. The elements of a safety management system have been proposed by the Health and Safety Executive [HSE 92].

16.1.5   Development of Culture

A safety management system provides an infrastructure to facilitate a continuing safety analysis. However, safety is not achieved because rules decree it, but because people set out to achieve it. A safety management system provides the rules, but a safety culture is the surest guarantee of achievement. If HAZOP is to be effective in improving the safety of the system under study, the technique needs to be employed within a safety culture. Culture may be defined as 'the way we do things here' [Levene 97] and, in the context of safety, implies (at least) an awareness of safety issues, a genuine desire and persistent effort to improve safety, and rapid action to remove any threat to safety. Yet, if hazard identification has not previously been formally carried out, it is unlikely that a safety culture exists in an organisation which is about to introduce HAZOP. Almost certainly, therefore, there is a need for a cultural change.

But changing culture is not trivial. It requires, among other things, leadership from the top, the commitment of senior management, a planned approach, and time. It is not our purpose here to describe how a culture change may be effected — for this, readers are referred to other relevant literature, such as [Levene 97]. But we do advise management to commission an objective examination of their organisation's culture and to plan and implement such improvements as are necessary to bring about a genuine safety culture. Only then are they likely to obtain the full, cost-effective benefits of HAZOP.

16.1.6   Infrastructure

It will have been seen from the earlier chapters of this book that successful HAZOP depends not merely on a study team, but on a number of other people besides — for example, the study initiator and the managers of the team members.

It may be possible to have a single study initiator in an organisation (though this does not allow for his absence), but it is not feasible to assume that the same study leader and team members will form all study teams. For the smooth running and success of HAZOP, an organisational infrastructure needs to be created.

One aspect of this falls under the heading of culture, which should cover such issues as:

- The acceptance by senior management of the cost of HAZOP. The most cost-effective way of achieving safety is to identify hazards early so as to plan how to deal with them. If money is 'saved' by carrying out an ineffective HAZOP, it becomes a great deal more expensive when rectification has to be made later.

- The willingness of managers to release staff to be HAZOP team members when they are required and if they possess the appropriate credentials.

Other aspects of the necessary infrastructure may require adjustments in the organisation itself. Examples are as follows.

A pool of study leaders may need to be created. Sometimes a number of people are trained but never used as study leaders, because their training is unknown to others such as study initiators. A formal structure needs to be created, in which careful selection is made of those to be trained and, when trained, the placing of their names and credentials on a register of potential study leaders.

An independent assessor, or auditor, may need to be appointed and trained to audit HAZOP. Or, an existing audit facility within the organisation might be extended for the purpose. In either case, the new responsibilities and authority should be explicitly defined.

Then, if improvement of the way in which HAZOP is carried out within the organisation is to be taken seriously (see Section 16.3), an infrastructure for inviting and receiving suggestions, and for planning, carrying out and monitoring improvements, also needs to be put in place.

A final example is making provision for the logistics of HAZOP meetings. This is often overlooked, but a small firm, without a great deal of spare accommodation, can find a HAZOP compromised if advance provision has not been made for study accommodation, refreshments, and so on (see Section 8.7).

The above is intended to remind management that the success of HAZOP does not depend only on 'technical' matters. In introducing the technique, management should consider their organisation's full infrastructure. Then, if HAZOP at first seems unsuccessful, they should not neglect to investigate infrastructure issues as well as technical ones. Cramped, noisy accommodation can have as demoralising an effect on a study team as can a deficient design representation. The importance of an appropriate working environment has been identified by DeMarco and Lister [DeMarco 87].

16.1.7   Introduction as a Project

In the previous sections it has been shown that the successful introduction
of HAZOP requires careful management. Necessary requirements include:
acquiring a thorough understanding of the technique, planning the whole
introduction process, specifying what is to be done, communicating with
staff, organising training, carrying out the introduction of the technique,
and monitoring and improving the process. This amounts to project
management [Redmill 88a]. It is recommended that introduction should
be treated by management as a project, with a project manager being
appointed to oversee the process. It should be planned carefully, managed
well, executed meticulously, and then reviewed regularly and thoroughly.

16.2 AUDITING

The application of a technique new to an organisation should always be
monitored, so as to measure the efficiency and effectiveness of its
application and to identify any needs for improvement. When the technique
is crucial to safety, as HAZOP is, it should be subject to formal audits, both
in its introduction and later when it is in regular use. There are two main
purposes of audit:

- To review the quality of the study process;
- To review the results of a particular study.

Reviewing the quality of the study process is checking its efficiency and
adherence to the organisation's rules. Criteria of such an audit might
include checking that:

- There were rules which the HAZOP should have adhered to, and
  that those rules were adhered to (including rules regarding the
  duration of meetings);
- The scope and objectives of the study had been clearly defined by
  the study initiator;
- The study leader had been trained;
- The credentials of team members were appropriate to the study;
- The managers of the most appropriate (originally selected) team
  members released the team members for participation in the study;
- The design representations used were appropriate to the objectives
  of the study and adequate for their purpose;
- Planning and other preparatory work had been carried out;

- The quality of the design representation had been assured prior to the study;
- Recording was carried out in accordance with the style defined by the study initiator;
- Every hazard, question and recommendation in the recorded output was individually numbered and labelled;
- All follow-up work which needed to be fed back to the study was carried out, fed back, acted on, and signed-off;
- If an extra follow-up meeting was held, its results were properly documented and signed-off.

Auditing the results of the study implies checking for effectiveness. Thus, the auditors may need to recruit appropriate experts to examine the design representation and the study documentation in the light of criteria such as the following:

- All entities had been identified and listed for study, and were studied;
- All attributes of each entity had been identified and were studied;
- Appropriate guide words had been identified for each attribute and were applied adequately during the study;
- A sample of system hazards identified by the auditor were found in the study.

The above criteria are examples only. It is the responsibility of an organisation to set its own criteria in accordance with its objectives for HAZOP in general or for a particular study.

Audits should be seen to be independent of the HAZOP study teams and, indeed, of anyone having an interest in the study, so it is recommended that an organisation should have an independent auditor to carry them out. In practice, it is often the Quality Assurance department which organises them. On some occasions the auditor should attend the study, or a number of study meetings, as an observer, and audit the manner in which the study is carried out. On other occasions, it may be sufficient to base the audit on the study documentation, checking the above criteria (and others) from it, and also that the documentation itself is complete, legible, and unambiguous, and that the objectives of the study were met.

16.3 PROCESS IMPROVEMENT

16.3.1   What Improvement?

HAZOP is unlikely to be employed to its full potential when first introduced into an organisation. Its exponents need time to understand its subtleties as well as its overt rules and attributes, and to become practised in its use. Study leaders need time to gain experience in what makes for an efficient study and what makes for an inefficient one, as well as in how to accelerate the process of building a team and maintaining its harmony, creativity and productivity. Designers need time to discover how deficiencies in design representations inevitably cause inefficient studies.

Improvement is a part of the normal introduction process and will occur naturally if management remain involved and committed, if training is carried out, and if the development of a safety culture continues, with the place of HAZOP in it being understood by everyone. But even after this 'bedding in' process, HAZOP can and should be subjected to continuous improvement. So what is it that we should be aiming to improve?

- The efficiency of the process — so as to save time and money;
- The effectiveness of the process — so as to find more hazards and thus achieve safer systems.

If we are to improve, we need to make the use of HAZOP more efficient and effective than previously — which means that we have to be able to measure the efficiency and effectiveness of our use of the technique. We need to carry out measurements, maintain the records, analyse them and determine the efficiency and effectiveness of each study — from which we can determine where improvement is necessary. We also need to plot trends over time, and from such trends determine whether improvement is being achieved.

However, as we shall see, it is not easy to determine what to measure or how our measurements will provide an unambiguous guide to efficiency and effectiveness or their improvement. They may even be misleading. Indeed, measurement for process improvement in HAZOP is not a mature subject. It has hitherto not received much consideration, and it is a subject which we propose as a candidate for serious research. We know of no research in this field, nor of any organisations which have attempted such an improvement process. So what follow are ideas and suggestions rather than a plan. Managers need to devise their own improvement programmes.

16.3.2   Efficiency and Effectiveness

The number of entities, or attributes, or attribute-guide-word combinations studied per person-hour at a meeting might provide a first indication of efficiency. But caution is required. Suppose that we fail to identify hazards because we have set too fast a pace, or because our thoughts are on speed rather than finding hazards. What good is speed of progress if hazards are not found?

Similarly, it may be thought that the number of hazards found per person-hour may be taken as a measure of effectiveness. But then, in a particularly difficult study (perhaps because the design representation is complex) the rate of discovery of hazards may justifiably be low. So, rate on its own may not be a consistent measure, and other circumstances need to be taken into consideration.

Perhaps the total number of hazards identified — in a study or meeting — would be a better guide to effectiveness. But then, in some systems, there may not be many different hazards, and the objective really is to find as high a proportion of those that exist. So comparing the number found in one study with that in another would be meaningless — or misleading. Further, since it cannot be known how many hazards exist, it is not possible to judge, for a single study, what proportion was found. However, it is possible to determine the number of hazards identified over a certain part of a system's life cycle — say, during development, or during development and for the first six months of operation — and then, retrospectively to determine what proportion of them was identified during a particular HAZOP. This does not provide immediate results but is a long-term improvement mechanism.

Then, there is the consideration of whether a hazard is major or minor. In the case of any given system, there should be a feel for the category of the worst possible hazards, and, in monitoring the process, notice should be taken of whether such hazards are indeed found. If at the end of a study no hazard which could result in the worst known consequence has been found, then it is likely that the study has not been as effective as it could have been.

Note also that the metrics used in the discussions of efficiency and effectiveness above were per person-hour rather than per hour. Clearly, if at two meetings the same number of attribute-guide-word combinations are studied in an hour, the more efficient study is that with fewer team members. So efficiency is not merely a function of time, but of both people and time. Yet, here too there needs to be a word of caution. Comparing efficiencies in this way assumes that the teams are properly constituted in the first place and that they are adequately led. Otherwise, a deduction would be that the most efficient team was a one-person team; and a superficial use of this line of analysis would lead to efficiency being attributed to teams which have been swift because the team members were not capable of identifying hazards. As emphasised throughout this book, the strength of HAZOP lies in teamwork as opposed to individualism. What is important in finding hazards (effectiveness of the process) is that appropriate team members are present and that they are well led so that their study identifies the deep hazards as well as the superficial ones.

So efficiency and effectiveness need to be taken together, and it should be recognised that an increase in one may be at the expense of a decrease in the other. In summary, there are at least three dimensions to be considered in monitoring HAZOP:

- The speed and cost of carrying out the HAZOP;
- The number of hazards found, or the number found per unit of time;
- The 'size' of hazards — it is important that the 'big' ones are found.

In monitoring any study, all of these should be considered, and the manner in which any one affects the others in the system under study should be taken into account.

A note is appropriate here on the number of hazards found. Hazards are the potential for danger, and such potential exists whether or not a countermeasure has been put in place. Thus, if it is suggested that, in measuring effectiveness, fewer hazards will be found if the designers have been safety-conscious, the point has been missed. As has been recommended in Chapter 9, hazards should not be ignored if countermeasures are in place; they should be recorded, and so their discovery should be recognised in the monitoring process. However, as suggested in Section 16.3.4, a measure of the 'safeness' of the design could be the ratio of the number of identified hazards which are already protected against to the total number of identified hazards.

One point on the collection of data is also worth making. The data from which many metrics may be derived is recorded as a normal part of any HAZOP and may be extracted from the meeting documentation. It is their use for process improvement which needs to be added to the basic technique.

16.3.3 Use of Measurements for Process Improvement

When an organisation begins to take measurements, the metrics only provide information about a single study, or study meeting — the one from which they are derived. However, over time, if the results from all meetings are collected at a single point (say, the organisation's 'HAZOP improvement team'), derived results of two types may be obtained:

- Organisation norms;
- Trends.

From the latter, changes (improvements or otherwise) in efficiency and effectiveness may be deduced, and these may be associated with previously taken actions or with the need for future actions. From the former, exceptional deviations (which should be investigated) can be detected. The general process is described by Redmill in another context [Redmill 88b].

Exceptional deviations from an organisation's norms may be in either direction — i.e. better or worse than the organisation norm. Further, an extremely efficient study may be found to have been ineffective, or vice versa. But a certain minimum level of efficiency and effectiveness should be expected, for HAZOPs are costly.

At the same time, monitoring alone will seldom bring about improvement, and it often needs to be followed by an investigation into something which the monitoring has highlighted. Thus, between monitoring and action, an investigation may be required. An investigation by a HAZOP expert of a suspect study should be carried out when, for example:

- A significant deviation of a metric from the organisation's norm is detected;
- The minimum level of efficiency or effectiveness set by the organisation is not met.

If on investigation an anomaly is found to be due to a deficiency in the process, appropriate action should be taken to improve it. Consider two examples: if investigation of an inefficient study reveals that there was too much extraneous discussion, action might take the form of retraining the study leader. Or, if it is found that inefficiency was due to deficiencies in the design representation, action might be the introduction of a mandate (perhaps an organisation standard) that design representations should be signed-off by a senior design authority before being used as the basis of a HAZOP. It should be remembered, however, that all deviations from the norm, even serious ones, do not necessarily indicate a problem. An investigator needs to recognise that there are sometimes exceptions — occasions when a deviation has a valid cause, such as when the study was of a complex design representation in an unfamiliar notation.

On the subject of action, there is also need for caution. If the trust of HAZOP participants is to be won, monitoring of the process should not be used against them, either in apportioning blame or in discrediting or embarrassing them. Instead, the culture needs to be developed in which everyone wishes the process to be improved, and everyone perceives metrics as a means by which they too can personally improve.

A good way to determine where improvement is necessary and, often, how it may be brought about, is to get feedback directly from the people who use HAZOP. It is therefore a good idea to install and maintain a feedback mechanism. If management were known to be receptive to ideas, and staff were comfortable in approaching them, a formal mechanism might not be necessary. But such open and effective vertical communication in an organisation is rare (though management usually likes to believe otherwise), so it is as well to introduce a mechanism for receiving comments on HAZOP from staff. This may take the form of a suggestion box for anonymous remarks, a formal means for the team members to criticise or score each study or study meeting at the time, providing a central point within the organisation to which comments should be addressed, or having a responsible person interview staff who have participated in a study. Whatever the means of acquiring feedback, staff should be given evidence that their suggestions are considered, taken seriously, and implemented if appropriate; and when they are not implemented, the staff should be informed why. In other words, feedback should, in return, be given to the staff.

We are not aware of any information publicly available on the expected values of HAZOP metrics, as few organisations are known to have carried out metric-based monitoring of the process. So an organisation will need to establish its own norms. What is certain is that whatever the initial values of metrics, improvement will be possible, so a determination to improve will be rewarded — if it includes the following:

- Leadership from the top;
- Taking measurements which have been chosen for their usefulness;
- Plotting the measurement over time;
- Establishing organisation norms;
- A determination to improve the norms;

- Monitoring trends in both efficiency and effectiveness;
- Linking efficiency and effectiveness and not taking either in isolation (beware that increasing one may decrease the other);
- Investigating significant deviations;
- Taking appropriate action when investigation reveals process deficiencies.

16.3.4   Some Suggestions

All aspects of HAZOP may be subjected to monitoring, but given the emphasis that we have placed on the control of the process, it is worth mentioning this aspect in the context of process improvement. The success of a study depends to a large extent on the study leader, so in many cases monitored deficiencies will be attributable to this person and remedial action may be to replace him or her. Thus, it is worth making a point of monitoring the efficiency and effectiveness of the study leader in addition to considering statistics relating directly to hazards and the rate of progress. For example, the rate of team building will have an effect on both the efficiency and the effectiveness of a study. So the number of items studied and the number of hazards identified per person-hour, from meeting to meeting, can, over the first few meetings, be a useful indicator of the development of the team. And this can be compared with the equivalent figures from other studies. Differences from organisation norms may indicate a deficiency in the study leader, and if that leader's statistics are compared with those of study leaders of known pedigree, conclusions may be drawn as to what action is necessary.

Another consideration is the 'goodness' of the design representation, which is important, for it can be the cause of variations in the efficiency of a HAZOP. Two factors which may affect 'goodness' are completeness and complexity.

A first indication of design goodness might be the number of questions documented at a meeting or in a study. If a design is incomplete it is likely to give rise to more questions; similarly, if it is particularly complex — in which case it may be excessively error prone and, thus, more likely also to include hazards.

Further, the 'safeness' of a design may be indicated by the ratio of the number of identified hazards which are shown already to be protected against to the total number of identified hazards. But, of course, this depends on the stage at which the HAZOP is carried out. It cannot be a valid measure when a preliminary hazard analysis is being carried out and can be realistic only if used when it is a complete design that is being studied.

The above are proposals only and do not constitute a plan for HAZOP process improvement. The main points are that the process can always be improved, it is worth improving, and there are ways in which it can be improved.

16.4 CONCLUDING REMARKS

The introduction of HAZOP into an organisation should be seen not as an event but as a process. Like any important process, it should be carefully planned, managed, executed, and then reviewed. Indeed, it should be treated as a project and a project manager appointed to control it.

Once HAZOP is in regular use, it needs to be regularly audited — to ensure that it is being carried out both efficiently and effectively, as a means of identifying any need for improvements in the way that it is carried out, and to assure the hazard identification and analysis process. Further, once the need for improvement of the application of HAZOP has been identified, appropriate courses of action should be devised, planned, implemented and monitored. If the safety of the system under study depends on the technique, then improvement of the technique will improve the chance of achieving a safe system.

This chapter has provided advice on introducing HAZOP and auditing and improving its use. The way in which any of these activities is undertaken depends on the nature of the organisation, so prescriptive instructions have not been given. Rather, guidance has been offered, and it is the responsibility of an organisation's management to decide how to use this guidance and how to integrate it into their own mode of operation.

References

[Annett 71]
> Annett J, Duncan K D, Stammers R B and Gray M J: *Task analysis: Training Information Paper No. 6*. HMSO, London, 1971

[BSI 91a]
> *BS 5760 Part 5: Guide to Fault Mode and Effects and Criticality Analysis (FMEA and FMECA)*. British Standards Institution, UK, 1991

[BSI 91b]
> *BS 5760 Part 7: Guide to Fault Tree Analysis*. British Standards Institution, UK, 1991

[CCL 95]
> *Public Report of the SADLI Project: Safety Assurance in Diagnostic Laboratory Imaging, March 1995*. Information Engineering Advanced Technology Programme, Reference IED 4/1/9042. Available from Cambridge Consultants Limited

[CIA 77]
> *A Guide to Hazard and Operability Studies*. Chemical Industries Association Limited, first published in 1997 and reprinted in 1992

[Cullen 90]
> The Hon. Lord Cullen: *The Public Inquiry into the Piper Alpha Disaster* (Cullen Report). HMSO, London, 1990

[DeMarco 87]

DeMarco T and Lister T: *Peopleware*. Dorset House, New York, 1987

[DOD 93]

MIL-STD-882C: System Safety Program Requirements. Department of Defense, USA, 1993

[Fencott 94]

Fencott P C and Hebbron B D: *The Application of HAZOP Studies to Integrated Requirements for Control Systems*. Proceedings of SAFECOMP '94, Anaheim, USA, October 1994

[HASAW 74]

UK Health and Safety at Work Act. HMSO, London, 1974

[Hatley 88]

Hatley D J and Pirbhai I A: *Strategies for Real-Time System Specification*. Dorset House, New York, 1988

[HSE 89]

Risk Criteria for Land Use Planning in the Vicinity of Major Industrial Hazards. HMSO, UK, 1989

[HSE 92]

Health and Safety Executive: *Successful Health and Safety Management*. Health and Safety Series Booklet HS(G) 65, second impression, HSE, 1992

[IEC 98]

Draft Standard IEC 61508: Functional Safety of Electrical/Electronic/ Programmable Electronic Safety-related Systems. International Electrotechnical Commission, Geneva, 1998

[ISO 94]

ISO 9000-1 to ISO 9000-4: *Quality Management and Quality Assurance Standards — Part 1 to Part 4*. International Organization for Standardization, Geneva, 1994 to 1997

[Jones-Lee 95]

Jones-Lee M W and Loomes G: Measuring the Benefits of Transport Safety. In: Redmill F and Anderson T (eds), *Achievement and Assurance of Safety — Proceedings of the Fourth Safety-critical Systems Symposium, Brighton 1995*. Springer Verlag, London, 1995

[Kirwan 92]

Kirwan B and Ainsworth L K: *A Guide to Task Analysis*. Taylor and

Francis, London, 1992

[Kletz 92]

Kletz T A: *HAZOP and HAZAN*. Institution of Chemical Engineers, UK, 1992

[Levene 97]

Levene T: Getting the Culture Right. In: Redmill F and Dale C (eds), *Life Cycle Management for Dependability*. Springer-Verlag, London, 1997

[Mason 97]

Mason S: Procedural Violations — Causes, Costs and Cures. In: Redmill F and Rajan J (Eds), *Human Factors in Safety Critical Systems*. Butterworth-Heinemann, Oxford, 1997

[McDermid 94]

McDermid J A and Pumfrey D J: *A Development of Hazard Analysis to Aid Software Design*. 9th Annual Conference on Computer Assurance, Gaithersburg, MD, USA. IEEE, June 1994

[McDermid 95]

McDermid J A, Nicholson M, Pumfrey D J and Fenelon P: *Experience with Application of HAZOP to Computer Based Systems*. 10th Annual Conference on Computer Assurance, Gaithersburg, MD. IEEE, June 1995

[MOD 95]

Draft Defence Standard 00-56: Safety Management Requirements for Defence Systems Containing Programmable Electronics. Ministry of Defence, UK, 1995

[MOD 96]

Interim Defence Standard 00-58 — HAZOP Studies on Systems Containing Programmable Electronics. Ministry of Defence, UK, 1996

[Reason 90]

Reason J T: *Human Error*. Cambridge University Press, UK, 1990

[Redmill 88a]

Redmill F: *The Introduction, Use and Improvement of Guidelines*. Proceedings of SAFECOMP '88 (Ed: Ehrenberger W D), Pergamon Press, Oxford, 1988

[Redmill 88b]

Redmill F, Johnson E A and Runge B: Documentation Quality — Inspection. *British Telecommunications Engineering Journal*, Vol 6 Part 4,

January 1988

[Redmill 97]
Redmill F, Chudleigh M F and Catmur J R: Principles Underlying a Guideline for Applying HAZOP to Programmable Electronic Systems. *Reliability Engineering and System Safety*, Vol. 55 No. 3, March 1997

[Sanders 93]
Sanders M S and McCormick E J: *Human Factors in Engineering and Design*. McGraw-Hill, New York, 1993

[Schreiber 93]
Schreiber G, Wielinga B and Breuker J: *KADS — A Principled Approach to Knowledge Based System Development*. Academic Press, London, 1993

[Shlaer 92]
Shlaer S and Mellor S: *Object Lifecycles: Modelling the World in States*. Yourdon Press, New York, 1992

[Storey 96]
Storey N: *Safety-Critical Computer Systems*. Addison-Wesley, London, 1996

[Westrum 91]
Westrum R. *Technologies and Society*. Wadsworth Inc., USA, 1991

Glossary

Accident
An unintended event or series of events that results in death or injury, or damage to property or the environment.

Attribute
A property or characteristic of an entity; it could be logical or physical.

Component
A discrete part of a total system, considered from the point of view of a particular level of analysis. At the lowest level of analysis, a component is a simple, discrete item; at higher levels, it may be complex, i.e. it may consist of sub-components. A component may be hardware, software, human, mechanical, electrical or electronic.

Design intent
The required or specified behaviour, or range of behaviours, of an aspect (usually an attribute) of the design of a system, as intended by the designer.

Design representation
A descriptive model of the design of a system or part of a system, presented according to a convention (for example, block diagrams, data flow

diagrams, or state transition diagrams). Here, 'design' is not limited to an abstract representation of logical design, but may include implementation details, physical details, environmental details and operating instructions; it is a description of the system under study.

Deviation
An excursion from its design intent of the value of an entity's attribute.

Entity
On a design representation, there are items at various hierarchical and logical levels, of which three are of interest in a HAZOP. At the first level there are the system components and the interconnections between them. At the next level are the entities which are possessed by the components and interconnections. Finally there are the attributes of the entities. As an example, if a component is a PES, one of its entities is its processing unit which possesses the attribute of 'throughput'. An interconnection between components may carry entities such as 'data' and 'control data' both of which may possess the attributes 'value' and 'bit rate'. As it is the attributes which are examined in a HAZOP, and the components and interconnections which are displayed on a design representation, 'entity' is a necessary intermediary in the identification of attributes.

Event
An occurrence which originates in a system or the system's operating environment.

Failure
The inability to exhibit behaviour, in given conditions, according to stated or implied requirements. In the case of a system or component, failure implies an inability to fulfil operational requirements.

Function
A defined feature of the intended behaviour of a system.

Guide word
A word or phrase which defines a particular deviation from design intent.

Hazard
A situation which has the potential to lead to harm.

Hazard analysis
An analysis or series of analyses to identify and determine the causes and consequences of hazards.

Hazard identification
The process of identifying hazards. In the context of this book, it is carried out to discover the hazards posed by a system. For best effectiveness, hazard identification requites a formal, well managed study using a technique such as HAZOP.

HAZOP
A formal systematic examination, by a team under the management of a trained leader, of the design intentions of a new or existing system or parts of a system, to identify hazards, mal-operation or mal-function of individual entities within the system and the consequences on the system as a whole and on its environment. It typically includes several HAZOP meetings.

HAZOP meeting
A meeting, chaired by the HAZOP study leader and carried out according to formal rules as part of the HAZOP process, when the study team meets to carry out the examination of one or more design representations.

Interconnection
A logical or physical link between two system components (at whatever level of analysis) which is defined by an interaction between the components and therefore exists because of the interaction.

Operability
The capacity of a system (which may include a human operator) to function. In this book, assumptions are made that a system is operable and that operators, where necessary, are able to use it effectively.

Procedure
A set of activities which need to be carried out in a defined order and according to defined rules.

Programmable electronic system (PES)
A system based on computer technology which may comprise hardware, software, and input and output devices.

Random Event
An event, ocurring randomly in time, which can result from a variety of degradation mechanisms.

Requirement
A statement which describes a need (e.g. an aspect of functional behaviour or performance) to be placed on a system and its operating environment.

Risk
The combination of the probability and the consequence of a hazardous event. In engineering, when numerical values of these two components are available, risk is taken to be their product, unless the criteria used to judge the acceptability of risk require that a different method of combining them be used. Otherwise, qualitative assessments may be combined in other ways.

Safety
Freedom from hazards which could lead to death or injury to people or damage to equipment, property, or the environment.

Safety analysis
An analysis, or series of analyses, whose purpose is to assess the safety of a system and its surroundings.

System
An organised set of complementary, interacting parts, which achieves in its environment a defined objective as the result of the properties, capabilities and behaviours of both the parts and their interactions.

Systematic event
An event which is repeatable if the same conditions re-occur. Such an event may be caused, for example, by faults in the specification, design or construction of a system, and may result from the combination of the fault and a given set of inputs. Software failures are systematic events. All system events that are not random are systematic.

Technique
The application of a technology, usually via a defined method.

Index

Printed and bound by CPI Group (UK) Ltd, Croydon, CR0 4YY

27/10/2024

14580206-0001